PUBLIC ENTERPRISE AND INCOME DISTRIBUTION

Other books by the same author:

Public Enterprise and the Developing World (Ed.), Croom Helm, 1983.
The Nature of Public Enterprise, Croom Helm, 1984.
Privatisation in the UK (Ed.), Routledge, 1988.

PUBLIC ENTERPRISE AND INCOME DISTRIBUTION

V.V. RAMANADHAM

ROUTLEDGE
London and New York

First published in 1988 by
Routledge
a division of Routledge, Chapman and Hall
11 New Fetter Lane, London EC4P 4EE

Published in the USA by
Routledge
a division of Routledge, Chapman and Hall, Inc.
29 West 35th Street, New York NY 10001

© 1988 V.V. Ramanadham

Printed and bound in Great Britain by
Biddles Ltd, Guildford and King's Lynn

All rights reserved. No part of this book may be reprinted or
reproduced or utilized in any form or by any electronic, mechanical, or
other means, now known or hereafter invented, including photocopying
and recording, or in any information storage or retrieval system, without
permission in writing from the publishers.

British Library Cataloguing in Publication Data

Ramanadham, V.V.
　Public enterprise and income distribution.
　1. Income. Distribution role of public
　enterprise
　I. Title
　ISBN 0-415-00916-2

Library of Congress Cataloging-in-Publication Data

Ramanadham, V.V. (Venkata Vemuri), 1920–
　public enterprise and income distribution / V.V. Ramanadham.
　　p. cm.
　Bibliography: p.
　Includes index.
　ISBN 0-415-00916-2
　1. Public investments. 2. Government business enterprises.
3. Income distribution. I. Title.
HC79.P83R36　　1988
339.2–dc19
　　　　　　　　　　　　　　　　　　　　　　　88-18258
　　　　　　　　　　　　　　　　　　　　　　　CIP

To my teacher
Professor Sir Arnold Plant

Contents

List of Figures	ix
List of Tables	x
Preface	xi

1. The Nature of the Problem — 1
The plan of the study — 1
Introductory background — 3
Appendix 1.1 State ownership in key sectors in Latin American countries — 10
Appendix 1.2 Major state-owned enterprises (SOE) in Venezuela — 12

2. Employee Incomes — 13
High wages — 13
Surplus labour — 17
Generous incentives — 21
Social expenditures — 22
Distributional implications — 25
A specific input policy — 32
Appendix 2.1 Wages in Kenyan public enterprises: an illustrative note — 33
Appendix 2.2 Public enterprise proportions in employment and wage earnings in Peru (1974–9) — 45
Appendix 2.3 Ancillaries assisted by public enterprises in India — 46

3. Pricing — 47
General observations — 47
Prices for final consumers — 49
Prices of intermediate goods — 56
Sectoral pricing — 58
Regional development policies — 63
Appendix 3.1 Cross-subsidizations in a monolithic enterprise: a case study — 67

Contents

4. **Deficits and Surpluses**	83
The nature of deficits	83
The effects	84
Direct budget expenditures	87
5. **The Aggregate Effects**	90
The size of the public enterprise sector	90
The composition of the public enterprise sector	91
Appendix 5.1 Dualism in income distribution	93
6. **Privatization and Income Distribution**	95
Introduction	95
The sale implications	96
The exchequer implications	100
Long-term implications	104
7. **Conclusion**	107
A résumé	107
The government and distributional policies	108
The institutional aspects	110
Notes	114
Index	127

Figures

1.1	Public investments and the Gini coefficient	11
2.1	Rates of change in wage employment in public and private enterprise 1972–80 (%)	35
2.2	Sectoral spread of public sector and excess of wage earnings (1983)	37
2.3	Sectoral spread of public enterprise employment and wage differentials (1983)	38
2.4	Employment and earnings in the public sector (1983)	39
2.5	Wage employment by income brackets (1982)	42
2.6	Public enterprise (PE) proportions in employment and wage earnings in Peru (1974–9)	45
3.1	City and mofussil fares	69
3.2	Viability under uniform fares	79
5.1	Employment and incomes in the agricultural sector in twelve countries	94

Tables

1.1	Public investments and Gini coefficients of some developing countries	8
1.2	Public investments as percentages of total sectoral investments	9
1.3	State ownership in key sectors in Latin American countries	12
1.4	Major state-owned enterprises (SOE) in Venezuela	12
2.1	Pay of top executives — averages, medians, and quartiles (1969)	15
2.2	Managerial emoluments in India (Rs per annum)	16
2.3	Social overheads of public enterprises (India) (1974–5)	24
2.4	Wage emoluments in public enterprise in India	25
2.5	Average wage earnings in Kenya (K£)	34
2.6	Employment and wage earnings in the public sector (1983)	36
2.7	Distribution of wage employment (numbers) (1982)	41
3.1	Classification of operations by profitability (1986–7)	70
3.2	Some data on operations, division-wise (1986–7)	72
3.3	Earnings and certain operational indicators	75
3.4	Viability of operations	77
3.5	Divisional spread of subsidizing and subsidized services	81
6.1	Market premiums on shares	97

Preface

This is a study on the instrumentality of public enterprise in the implementation of national policies of income distribution. I used an early draft of it while delivering the Dr D.S. Reddi Memorial Lectures at Hyderabad, India, in 1980 at the kind invitation of the Osmania University. The script had undergone several substantive revisions as a result of discussions with professional friends in India, the United States of America, and the United Kingdom over the years, until I finalized it for publication while at Templeton College, Oxford.

V.V. Ramanadham
Oxford, April 1988

Chapter one

The Nature of the Problem

The plan of the study

The purpose of this study is to present an analytical review of the ways in which public enterprise may offer itself as an instrument in implementing national policies of income distribution. It does not contain a full-fledged discussion of the whole problem of income distribution. It proceeds on the assumption that the operations of public enterprises can play a part in the totality of measures applied in that field.

No attempt is made at an empirical review of the problem. The focus is on examining the theoretical potentialities of the different channels of impact by public enterprises on income distribution, the extent of their practicability, and the nature of limitations that qualify the use of a given channel.

The use of illustrative material, drawn from the developing countries as well as from the United Kingdom, is only intended to add realism to the discussion at certain points. Appendices 2.1 and 3.1 also have a similar purpose, by and large, and may be of additional interest from the technical angle of attempting an empirical review.

In the course of the discussion comments will be made, wherever appropriate contextually, on how a given public enterprise strategy compares with available alternatives of public policy in achieving an intended result.

While the discussion proceeds essentially in terms of personal incomes, references will be made to the impact of certain public enterprise operations on regional and sectoral incomes and some comments will be added on its relationship with the personal aspects of income distribution.

Reference will be made, at the appropriate places, to the administrative aspects of the public concerns that certain distributional channels of operations of public enterprises are likely to raise.

The discussions on wage incomes, pricing, and surpluses are confined to those aspects that are most directly linked with the distributional aspects of public enterprise operations.

The study does not go into such basic questions concerning income distribution as the following: whether and under what conditions distributional aims are preferable to growth aims; whether distributional justice and growth are simultaneously achievable and in what relative proportions; how far the adverse effects, if any, of distributional measures on savings and growth are to be accepted; and what kind of redistribution is the best for a society to aim at. Our hypothesis is that distributional measures in favour of the lower-income brackets of the population are desirable and our aim is to review how meaningful public enterprise can be as a vehicle in this regard.

While the major theme of the study relates to incomes, references will also be made at appropriate points to the distributional aspects of wealth.

The distributional impacts of a public enterprise will be reviewed under three headings, in the main: employee incomes; pricing; and surpluses. However, brief references will be made to allied aspects such as input policies.

Two levels of public enterprise may be distinguished for the purpose of the study. The first is that of an individual enterprise. The focus is on its distributional instrumentality; and the discussion is of no less relevance to a country with a relatively small public enterprise sector than to one which is relatively public enterprise-oriented. The other level is that of public enterprise as a whole. From its institutional nature, as well as from its relative size in the economy and sectoral composition, certain impacts could flow in the area of income and wealth distribution. These will also be pursued in the study.

It will be useful to indicate at the outset the questions that frequently arise, almost under every distributional channel considered in the study. First, who benefits from a given policy of a public enterprise which has distributional implications, and how do they stand in the context of the distributional policies of the nation? Second, who yields the benefit under a given policy of a public enterprise which has distributional implications, and how do they stand in the context of the distributional policies of the nation? Third, what are the immediate effects of a given channel of distributional impacts of public enterprise, and what are the subsequent rounds of effects? Can the latter be identified and how far can one go in doing so? Fourth, do alternative methods of achieving given distributional ends exist and are they preferable to the instrumentality of a public enterprise channel?

One final prefatory word on the plan of the study. We shall commence with an introductory backdrop delineating the importance of distributional aims in the development strategies of several countries, and the relative significance attributed to public enterprise as a means of development. The main analysis then follows, ranging over the distributional potentialities of a public enterprise through its policies regarding employee incomes, pricing and surplus. Next we shall discuss the impacts of public enterprise as an institution and its aggregate size on income and wealth distribution. This will be followed by an analysis of what effects privatization, which is widely in vogue, may have on income distribution. Finally there will be a brief conclusion relevant to public policy in the area of public enterprise and income distribution.

Introductory background

The purpose of this section is simply to present certain features of the development strategies of a large number of countries, which have relevance for the theme of distributional policies through the medium of public enterprise.

The distributional objectives

The first is that many developing countries have gradually[1] incorporated among the objectives of their development plans the attainment of a more equitable distribution of income (and wealth) than obtains today, as growth takes place.[2] Typically illustrative of this approach is the statement in the Fourth Plan of Pakistan that 'the nation may well have to accept a less ambitious growth target for the Fourth Plan in order to combine it with other social and economic objectives' such as 'reducing regional disparity and distributing incomes more equitably'.[3]

However, the formulation of the distributional objective is, on the whole, far from precise. Nigeria's recent observation that it 'has never had an articulate and deliberate incomes policy'[4] applies to many other countries as well.

The distributional emphasis in development strategies has been so common in developing countries that it would be of some interest to look at a wide range of excerpts from their plan documents with a view to understanding the nature of the emphasis.

> *Sri Lanka*: While the immediate social objective of the Plan is to provide employment, it also aims to bridge the present disparities in incomes and living standards by raising the incomes and living conditions of the low-income households.[5]
>
> *India*: One of the basic objectives of the plan is to raise the consumption levels of the lowest 30 per cent of our population.[6]
>
> A progressive reduction in the incidence of poverty and unemployment; strengthening the redistributive bias of public policies and services in favour of the poor, contributing to a reduction in inequalities of income and wealth; a progressive reduction in regional inequalities in the pace of development and in the diffusion of technological benefits.[7]

Iran: A secondary objective . . . to bring about a more even distribution of income among regions and social classes.[8]

To provide sufficient and appropriate encouragement for investment in regions with low rates of growth.[9]

Direct government investment in infrastructural facilities in rural areas.[10]

To place more emphasis on low-income groups in urban areas by the expansion of free government services and meeting the basic requirements of low-income groups at reasonable prices.[11]

Kuwait: To ensure a more equitable distribution of income in order to achieve a reasonable degree of social justice.[12]

Pakistan: To accelerate development of backward regions and their integration with more developed centres, through a favourable treatment of poorer Provinces in the allocation within Provincial Programmes as well as through investments in the Central Programme; to ensure availability of essential consumer goods and to minimize the adverse effects of inflation in the context of an equitable distribution of income.[13]

Malaysia: To correct the imbalances in the income distribution, employment and ownership, and control of wealth.[14]

Bangladesh: To reduce poverty . . . it requires an expansion of employment opportunities for the unemployed and underemployed. It also requires an acceleration in the rate of growth of national income, as well as effective fiscal and pricing policies for its equitable distribution; to expand the output of essential consumption items to provide the minimum consumption requirements of the masses; to ensure a wide and equitable diffusion of income and employment opportunities throughout Bangladesh.[15]

Afghanistan: Efforts to achieve a distribution of national income according to criteria of social justice and economic welfare.[16]

Jordan: Redistribution of public services and ensuring gains more properly among the different regions and the population groups.[17]

Tanzania: Social equality . . . . To spread the benefits of development widely throughout society; the development of forms of economic activity which encourage collective and co-operative efforts and avoid wide differences of wealth and income.[18]

Nigeria: More even distribution of income. Development is not just a matter of growth in *per capita* income. . . . An important objective is to spread the benefits of economic development so that the average Nigerian would experience a marked improvement in his standard of living.[19]

In the past the rural areas have lagged behind the urban areas in development resulting in increasing disparity between the standard of living in the rural and urban areas. With reference to income distribution the plan strategy adopted is for the public sector to provide subsidized facilities for the poorer sections of the population, including electrification, water supplies, health services, co-operatives, and community development programmes in the rural areas and housing in the urban areas for the low-income groups. These programmes will constitute a more practical means of income redistribution than other more direct measures.[20]

Ghana: Equitable distribution of income in terms of equal access to employment and productive opportunities.[21]

The quest for a fair and equitable distribution of income and wealth in our circumstances must be sought primarily in the provision of gainful employment for all Ghanaians who are willing and able to work.[22]

Uganda: Promoting a more equitable distribution of incomes and wealth among all sections of the nation's population, particularly through emphasis upon rural development; it will be the Government policy to make all basic social services available to those in the lowest-income brackets free of charge or at greatly subsidized rates of charges. It is now anticipated that, in their impact on farmers' income and consumer prices, [the public enterprises] will more effectively promote Government's income policy.[23]

Sierra Leone: Increase the welfare of the broad masses of population as the ultimate aim of development and to that end achieve more equitable distribution of wealth and income.[24]

Equity ... particularly important in case of enterprises rendering essential public utility services such as road transport and ... in the case of the Sierra Leone Produce Marketing Board.[25]

Somalia: Creating conditions where national product is distributed equitably among the people.[26]

Ecuador: To improve the conditions of living of the people of Ecuador, particularly of those sectors that are faced with absolute poverty and that constitute large social groups.[27]

Despite considerable diversity in the expressions of different governments on the distributional objectives of their plans, these excerpts have value in suggesting that:

(i) There is a fairly clear undercurrent in favour of sectoral and regional redistributions, and these are often understood to be a major means of dealing with the distributional inequities among persons.

(ii) An emphasis is discernible on making relatively cheap merit goods and services available to the poorer classes of people.

(iii) There is a positive thinking on the propriety of the physical objective of expanding certain kinds of goods or 'essentials', whose adequate availability is a vital step in effectuating distributional policies.

(iv) Stress is laid on the provision of employment opportunities as a basic step in dealing with the prevailing distributional inequities.[28]

(v) There is some reference in certain plans to the connection between the forms of economic organization on the one hand and the prospect of distributional measures on the other.

(vi) Specific targets in the realm of income (and wealth) redistribution are, on the whole, not common. (A few Plans illustrate the kind of targets that exist.)[29] Non-specificity in this regard contributes to complications both at the level of decisions on distributional policy and at the level of evaluation of distributional results.

The distributional preferences are so phrased in the plans of countries like India, Tanzania, Ghana, and Sierra Leone that the use of public enterprise as a vehicle of implementation suggests itself easily. Some emphatic references can be cited:

It was observed in a Presidential Circular in Tanzania that 'broad policy is a matter for the elected TANU Government of Tanzania, and the parastatal organizations are instruments of execution — tools which must be used by the policy makers'.[30] Likewise the Government of Zambia pronounced that 'those business organizations in which Government has a controlling share must become vehicles for carrying out the main policy objectives of the SNDP aimed at the diversification of the economy, the reduction of prices, the stabilization of the cost of living, and reducing the income and employment gap between rural and urban areas'.[31] Just another instance: having reorganized the public enterprise sector a few years ago, the Government of Uganda observed that 'it is now anticipated that, in their impact on farmers' incomes and consumer prices, these bodies will more effectively promote Government's incomes policy'.[32]

Malaysia offers clear evidence on the distributional purpose of public enterprise. A major objective of the New Economic Policy is the promotion of the economic well-being of the poorest section, namely, the Malays (or bumiputeras) by enlarging their incomes and property ownership in such a manner that their relative position records considerable improvement, as compared with the other ethnic groups (Indian and Chinese), and that their ownership of 'the total commercial and industrial activities of the economy in all categories and scales of operation' will reach 30 per cent, as compared with the 'mere 2 per cent of the overall total' ownership of share capital in the early 1970s.[33]

The problem

Finally reference may be made to a recent observation by the Government of India that one of 'the major objectives' of public enterprises is 'to promote redistribution of income and wealth'.[34]

The primacy of public enterprise investments

Another feature of development strategy adopted by many developing countries — closely relevant to our study — consists of the relatively high role assigned to public investments. Data for thirty-eight countries have been extracted from the national Plan documents and presented in table 1.1 in descending order in terms of percentages of public investments in the total investments (in column 2).

In six countries the absolute primacy of public, as against private, investments is clear — the former constituting three-quarters or more of the aggregate national investments; in eighteen others the proportion of public investments is 50 per cent or more, though below 75 per cent; and it is only in six of the reviewed thirty-eight countries that they fall below a third of the total investments in the Plan periods concerned.

These data certify the existence of a strong institutional background for distributional policies in those countries where public investments have been the most significant. The development strategy has implications for where the investments are located, what outputs are invested in, what managerial controls (over inputs, outputs, and prices) can emerge from the 'owners' (i.e. the government), and what profit targets may be aimed at by the individual projects invested in. In all these respects the government can aim to achieve the national goals of distributive justice.

There is one qualification to the data, which has to be noted in the context of our focus on public enterprise.

The public investments to which the data refer are not confined to public enterprises only; they cover governmental investments in other channels as well. It has not been easy to cull specific data indicating the relative extent of national investments specifically in public enterprises for all the countries covered by table 1.1. In most cases, however, public enterprises absorbed high proportions of the public investments. Some evidence is available from the detailed data in table 1.2 representing the planned share of public authorities in the total investments in certain sectors of activity during the recent Plan periods (the same as in table 1.1) in respect of some countries. The conclusion is clear, namely, that in sectors like transport and communications, power and other public utilities, mining and manufacturing, the role of public enterprises, as measured through the investment activity, is prominent.

These data, incidentally, have the value of suggesting that public enterprises have a high potential for pursuing policies harbouring

Table 1.1 Public investments and Gini coefficients of some developing countries

Country (1)	Percentage of public to total investments[1] (2)	Plan period (3)	Gini coefficient[2] (4)	Year (5)
75% and above				
Afghanistan	90	1972–7		
Bangladesh	89	1973–8	0.1730	1966– NL, POP
Syria	81	1971–5		
Nepal	77	1975–80		
Iraq	75	1970–4	0.6288	1956 NL, POP
Tanzania	71	1969–74	0.5973	1969 NL, HH
50–74%				
Bolivia	71	1976–80		
Botswana	67	1973–8	0.5740	1971–2 NL, EAP
Nigeria	67	1975–80		
India	66	1974–9	0.4775	1967–8 NL, HH
Iran	66	1973–8	0.5018	1968 URB, HH
Zambia	65	1972–6	0.5226	1959 NL, HH
Madagascar	62	1974–7		
Senegal	61	IV	0.5874	1960 NL, POP
Panama	60	1976–80	0.5567	1969, NL, EAP
Pakistan	60	1970–5	0.2076	1969–70 NL, POP
Peru	56	1975–8	0.5941	1970–1 NL, EAP
Morocco	55	1973–7		
Malawi	55[3]	1971–80	0.4696	1969 NL, HH
Chile	54	1980–1	0.5065	1968 NL, HH
Sudan	54	1970–5	0.4460	1963 A, HH
Venezuela	53	1976–80	0.6223	1971 NL, EAP
Jordan	50	1976–80		
Uganda	50[3]	1971–6	0.4007	1970 NL, A
34–50%				
Mauritius	49	1975–80		
Sri Lanka	47	1972–6	0.3530	1973 NL, HH
Sierra Leone	46	1975–8	0.6117	1968–9 A, HH
Argentina	42	1974–7	0.4375	1961 NL, HH
Dominican Republic			0.4928	1969 A, HH
Malaysia	41	1976–80	0.5407	1970 NL, PC
Nicaragua	40	1975–9		
Ecuador	40	1973–7	0.6826	1970 NL, EAP
Democratic Yemen	38	1974–9		
33% or below				
El Salvador	33	1973–7	0.4653	1969 NL, POP
Barbados	32	1977	0.4264	1969–70 NL, EAP
Costa Rica	30	1974–8	0.4445	1971 NL, HH
Korea	29	III	0.4065	1970 NL, POP
Uruguay	28	1973–7	0.4279	1967 NL, HH
Philippines[3]	19	1974–7	0.4941	1971 NL, HH

[1] As per the Plans.
[2] The World Bank, Shail Jain (1975) *Size Distribution of Income — A Compilation of Data*, Washington, DC.
[3] The figures refer to capital formation.
NL — National; POP — Population; HH — Household; URB — Urban; AG — Agriculture; IR — Income recipient; EAP — Economically active population.

Table 1.2 Public investments as percentages of total sectoral investments

Country	Transport and communications	Power and other utilities	Mining	Manufacturing	Total material production (agriculture, mining and manufacturing)
(1)	(2)	(3)	(4)	(5)	(6)
Iran	84.6	91.1	86.6	35.5	60.7
India	79.0	98.4	57.8		61.1
Bangladesh	90.7	100.0		84.2	91.5
Afghanistan	100.0	100.0	100.0	55.9	89.7
Nepal	75	77			70
Botswana	100.0	100.0		42.0	32.3
Nigeria	91.7	100.0	56.0	65.5	60.2
Mauritius	66.7		22.1		29.6
Sierra Leone	63.3	70.7	11.6	37.5	42.4
Senegal	45.6		6.8		61.2
Morocco	87.7	42.7			51.4
Ecuador	60.7	90.0	5.7	24.3	23.1
Venezuela	67.1	89.2	97.9	49.8	61.3
Bolivia	75.5	77.7	90.2	73.8	80.5
Costa Rica		100.0			
Nicaragua	100.0	100.0	2.2		17.5
Chile	47.1	100.0	61.2	31.5	42.2
Sierra Leone	63.3	70.7	11.6	37.5	42.4
Madagascar	100.0 (roads)	42.0 (inc. manufacturing)			62.2

United Nations, Committee for Development Planning (1977) *Planning for Development: Goals and Policies of Developing Countries for the Second Half of the 1970s*, Ch. I, table 1-12 (E/AC.54/L.91), New York.

distributional objectives. In several sectors they occupy positions of monopoly. Hence it is easy for them to adopt input and output strategies without being inhibited by the presence of competitors and without deference to market disciplines. Some illustrative data on the monopoly elements in the public sector are provided in table 1.3 which relates to many Latin American countries and in table 1.4 which indicates that ten out of the thirteen major public enterprises in Venezuela enjoy monopoly power.

In most developing countries income disparities and disparities in regional development have been so alarming that governments tended to look at public enterprise as an important weapon in their policy decisions aimed at dealing with them.

It is not easy to cite data for many countries on a comparable basis in respect of income disparities. One measure of the inequalities, the Gini coefficient,[35] is tabulated in column 4 of table 1.1 for those countries for which figures are found in a recent World Bank study; and the years to which they relate and the population to which they refer are shown in column 5. Using the data of table 1.1, it is difficult to generalize on the interrelationship between the relative size of public investments and income inequalities. The data relate to different years, and figures ranging as widely as 19 and 68 per cent, relating to public investments, are associated with the range of 0.4000–0.5000 of the Gini coefficient, as indicated in figure 1.1.

The scatter suggests a fit that slants upwards from the area of low public investment percentages and low Gini coefficients. (Bangladesh and Pakistan are glaring exceptions.) It is difficult to speculate on the precise meaning of the slant, except that there is some indication that many of the countries with high Gini coefficients followed strategies of relatively high public investment. The latter, it must be noted, was the product of many other factors, most importantly on the side of growth.

Figure 1.1 Public investments and the Gini coefficient

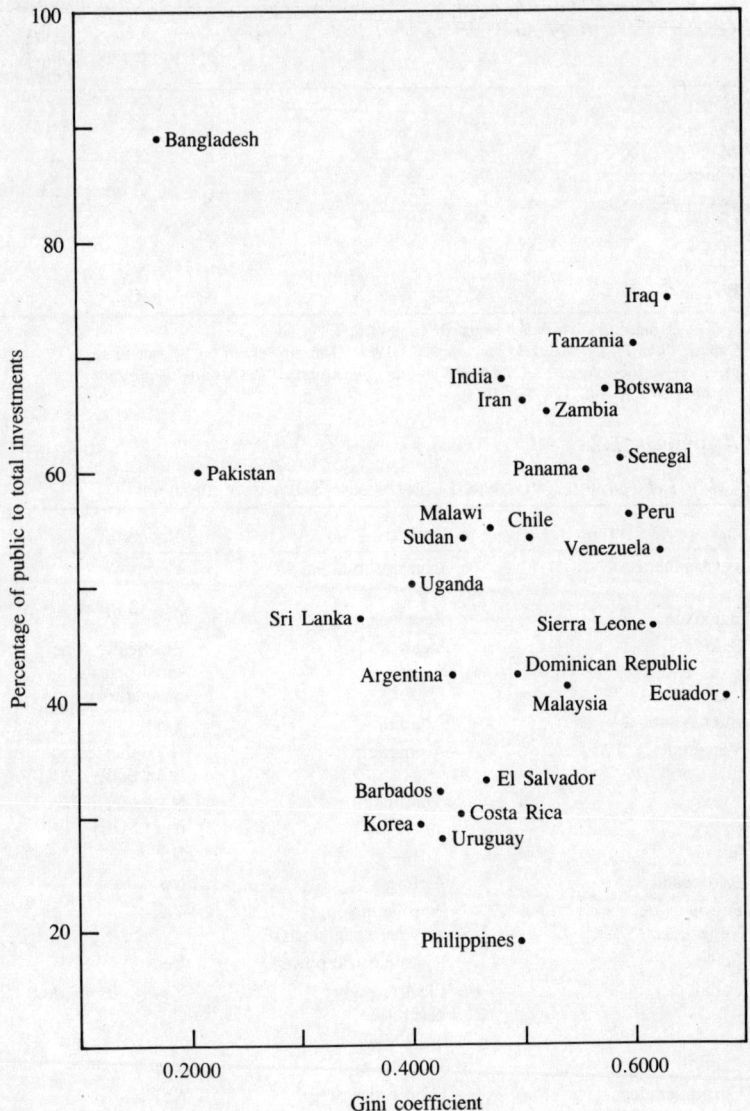

Appendix 1.1

Table 1.3 State ownership in key sectors in Latin American countries

Country	Electricity	Airlines	Mining	Steel	Railroads	Banking	Telephones	Petroleum	Food distribution
Brazil	X		X	X	X		X	X	X
Colombia	X		X	X	X		X	X	X
Mexico	X	X	X	X	X	X	X	X	X
Venezuela	X	X	X	X	X		X	X	X
Argentina	X	X		X	X		X	X	
Chile	X	X	X	X	X		X	X	
Peru	X	X	X	X	X		X	X	X
Ecuador	X	X			X		X	X	
Bolivia	X		X	X	X		X	X	

X denotes industries which are primarily in government hands.
Coburn, John F. and Wortzel, Lawrence H. (1984) 'The problem of public enterprise: is privatization the solution?', *Conference on State Shrinking: A Comparative Inquiry into Privatization*, Austin, TX, March.

Appendix 1.2

Table 1.4 Major state-owned enterprises (SOE) in Venezuela

State-owned enterprises	Activity	Monopoly?
Ferrominera	Iron ore mining, processing	Yes
Bauxiven	Bauxite mining	Yes
Sidor	Steel	Practically (one small private competitor)
Inter Alumina	Alumina	Yes
Venalum	Aluminium	No (other competitor is an SOE)
Alcasa	Aluminium	No (other competitor is an SOE)
Viasa	Airline	No
Aeropostal	Airline	No
Petróleos de Venezuela	Petroleum (oil, gas, petrochemicals)	Yes
Edelca	Hydroelectric power	Yes
Cadafe	Electric power generation, distribution	Yes (in its market)
Cantv	Telephones	Yes
Corpomeradeo	Food processing and distribution	No

Coburn, John F. and Wortzel, Lawrence H. (1984) 'The problem of public enterprise: is privatization the solution?', *Conference on State Shrinking: A Comparative Inquiry into Privatization*, Austin, TX, March.

Chapter two

Employee Incomes

Public enterprise policies on emoluments to employees are among the most direct of channels that have a distributional impact. These will be examined under four headings: high wages; surplus labour; generous incentives; and liberal social expenditures.

High wages

The basis for assuming that public enterprises offer 'high' wages is threefold. First, the government intends that they should be 'model employers'[1] and that the wage rates offered in public enterprise ought to have a demonstration effect on the rest of the economy. Second, a majority of public enterprises in several developing countries are characterized by some degree of monopoly power; hence the employees can exercise their muscle in wage negotiations.[2] Third, the employees derive a sense of political power, because of their relatively easy access to the political interests in government; and any prospect of a long drawn-out strike arouses parliamentary criticism which the ministers concerned want to avoid. In short, there develops an atmosphere of softness all round in the parcelling out of employee remunerations from out of the revenues of the enterprises.

The concept of 'high' wages in public enterprises, implying that the wages are higher than in private enterprises, calls for qualification. Higher wages would be possible under the following conditions:

(i) Where the public enterprise is a monopoly and the monopoly power is used by the workers to negotiate high wage levels without the fear of competing enterprises in the private sector wielding a contrary pull.

(ii) Where a public enterprise is located in a remote area. The tendency develops for the wage rates to contain an element of compensation for the hardships of location. This may be the only way of attracting workers to the site. Even private enterprises may have to do the same thing; but they hardly go into such areas, as long as choices of investment in other locations exist.

(iii) There can be an allied reason. Publicity gains for the idea that the location of a public enterprise in a remote or difficult area is meant to help raise the income potential of the area. Thus the enterprise is not impelled to take advantage of the local conditions of cheap supply of labour but offers wage rates that can be construed as 'high' in market terms.

(iv) Where public enterprises offer not necessarily higher wage levels, but conditions of service that effectively vary from and are superior to those in private enterprise, for example, leave privileges, retirement benefits and pension conditions.[3] When quantified, these raise the effective wage levels, though apparent similarities seem to prevail in so far as the basic wage rate schedules are concerned.

(v) Wage costs in terms of a unit of output or revenue tend to be higher in the public enterprise sector, though the wage rates are similar to those in comparable private enterprises for another reason, namely, that conditions of lower productivity characterize a large number of public enterprises. Thus the benefits of wage incomes per unit of output tend to be higher. This is not a doctrinaire observation; empirical support is ubiquitous. The many reports of the Committee on Public Undertakings (CPU) in India offer clear insights into this phenomenon.

Appendix 2.1, relating to Kenya, provides a good illustration of the proposition that wage incomes in public enterprise tend to be relatively high. Evidence on this tendency may be drawn from the Latin American region as well. Available data for Peru,[4] graphically presented in appendix 2.2, suggest that for a given percentage of labour proportion in the economy, public enterprises accounted for a higher proportion of all wage and salary payments, in the same way as in Kenya. (The equiproportional diagonal line facilitates the inference.)

Public enterprise policies and practices are, on the whole, generous in so far as the compensations to the employees in the lower emoluments cadres are concerned (the workers in particular, skilled as well as unskilled), whereas the compensations offered to the higher levels, for example, the managerial personnel, do not compare favourably with those in the private sector. One may infer from this phenomenon that the enterprises pursue policies that are restrictive of income accruals in favour of the higher brackets of earners, in contradistinction to favouring income accruals for the lower brackets.

An interesting reference may be made, at this point, to the aim enunciated in the *Draft Fifth Five Year Plan 1974–5* of India (p. 23): 'improvement of wage share to be brought about at the expense of the consumption of owners of property.' It is certain that such an overall aim has an impact on public enterprise wage determinations.

Employee incomes

Evidence on the disparities in compensation unfavourable to the managerial (or higher paid categories of) employees in public enterprise may be adduced from the experience of two countries — the United Kingdom and India.

In 1969 the National Board for Prices and Incomes enquired into top salaries in the private sector and nationalized industries in the United Kingdom and concluded that 'at all levels covered by the reference and immediately below, salaries prevailing in the nationalized industries are substantially lower than those obtaining in the private sector (although at lower levels this is not the case). Retirement benefits are also lower in the public sector, principally because pensions and gratuities are tied to lower final salaries.' These differences in total remuneration, that is pay and pensions combined, do not correspond with differences in the levels of responsibilities carried by senior managers in nationalized industries, as compared with men in similar positions in private sector industries, in so far as differences in responsibilities are measurable.[5] The data in table 2.1 support the Board's conclusion.[6] (It is interesting to refer to the Board's observation that 'the level of pay in the British Steel Corporation is substantially higher than in other State enterprises and reflects in part its recent past as a group of separate private enterprises').[7]

Data relating to 1987 continue to reflect the disparities in the top salaries in the public and private sectors. 'With few exceptions, the salary for a full-time nationalized industry Chairman is less than £80,000 a year.

Table 2.1 Pay[1] of top executives — averages, medians and quartiles (1969)

Category of executive	Nation- alized	Nationalized excluding British Steel	Sector of industry Private				
			Group A	Group B	Group C	Total	Financial
	£	£	£	£	£	£	£
Main board members							
Average	10,540	8,860	18,760	15,650	12,380	13,310	13,170
Median	9,290	8,910	16,480	14,720	11,590	12,210	12,170
Upper quartile	12,220	9,940	24,130	18,380	15,090	16,150	15,870
Lower quartile	8,080	7,890	12,810	12,340	9,050	9,700	9,650
Senior executives[2]							
Average	6,880	6,270	9,790	8,040	6,470	6,940	7,800
Median	6,520	6,330	9,090	7,910	6,240	6,650	7,320
Upper quartile	7,480	7,190	11,800	9,490	7,740	8,520	9,780
Lower quartile	5,560	5,470	7,410	6,450	5,080	5,320	5,550

[1] Pay includes salary, directors' fees, and bonus.
[2] Selected sample of executives in senior positions in the firms covered.

A job with equivalent responsibility in the private sector commands at least £150,000'.[8]

Of similar interest are data that indicate the steep hikes in top salaries on the privatization of a nationalized industry.[9]

That the top salaries in public enterprise in India are lower than in private enterprise can be deduced from such findings of the Administrative Reforms Commission as the following. 'Considering the need for recruiting the best available talent for manning the top posts in the public undertakings, it is essential that the salaries and conditions of service attaching to these posts are adequate and attractive'. The 'maximum limit of Rs4,000/- a month . . . should be enhanced'.[10]

More recent evidence comes from the CPU[11] which cited the following comparative figures on managerial emoluments as compiled by the Boothalingam Committee on Wages, Incomes, and Prices.

Table 2.2 Managerial emoluments in India (Rs per annum)

(1)	Central government (2)	Public sector (3)	Banks (4)	Private sector (5)
Salary (post-tax)	32,685	35,925	55,925	53,460
House, car, etc. Total (post-tax)	58,106	71,665	71,859	156,535

After the Fourth Pay Commission's recommendations, salaries of the top managers in the public sector have become lower than those of government secretaries; while comparable private sector salaries are nearly twice as high under the changes currently contemplated in company legislation.

Nigeria provides certain interesting insights into public thinking on the question of top salaries. The Working Party on Statutory Corporations and State-owned Companies[12] not only found through 'research' in 1966 that 'abnormal salary inflations at the top management level existed, sometimes through interenterprise competition' in the recruitment market, but even developed the theme that payment by public enterprises of 'salaries which are higher than those of the civil service' could 'hardly be justified'. It viewed with disfavour the analogy of salaries in the private sector 'where top salaries are based on the rates of pay for expatriate personnel who have to be induced to come out to Nigeria from countries like the United Kingdom'. It pointed out the 'historical factor' in the evolution of top salaries in public enterprise, namely, that they were originally 'fixed as fees for short-term contracts' and 'contained substantial elements of contract enhancement all of which have been inequitably inherited by indigenous successors who are on normal career terms'. The salary levels recommended by the Working Party reflected its clear bias for downward readjustments in the then prevailing salary structures in public enterprises.

Another significant aspect of the Working Party's views relates to 'the fantastic differentials between emoluments at the top and bottom levels in the large corporations'. These should be given 'serious consideration', it argued, 'since they are capable of disturbing social peace'.[13] Interestingly enough, the salary grades recommended in the Report implied, on the whole, a scaling down of the prevailing scales for the four top classes of managerial personnel and an upward scaling in respect of the bottom three classes.

In conclusion, for a proper perspective on the data on the emoluments of the top managers an important qualification is worth noting. They reflect the incomes policy angle in a sense, though the rationale of their relatively low level is question-begging in a mixed economy.

Surplus labour

A large number of public enterprises all over the world have been found to carry excessive staff, that is, they have on the rolls a bigger labour force than their operations justify. This has a distributional implication in countries with a high rate of unemployment and underemployment in that the enterprises place incomes in the hands of persons that otherwise might not be able to earn them, if thrown out. So while apparently earning a wage, a part of the labour force is virtually in receipt of a sheer distributional benefit.

The reasons why surplus labour is common in the public enterprise sector may be set out in the following terms.

(i) In many developing countries the activities entrusted to public enterprises are relatively new and the technologies are imported, so much so that, unless extreme caution is exercised, faulty and rather low work standards are established leading to the intake of more employees than are strictly necessary. The situation is often complicated by controversial assumptions on the 'efficiency factor' used to determine the exact number of workers needed in a developing country in a new technology industry for a given number that might be enough in the technology-exporting country. This kind of problem rarely arises in an industrially advanced country, where, therefore, nationalizations are on the whole followed by far less labour excessiveness than in the developing countries. (Significant exceptions exist, as will be noted later in this section.)

(ii) Public enterprises which need a large number of workers during the construction stages find it hard to disband them as production commences, when a smaller number as well as a different composition of skills is required. This happens the more certainly if the construction was undertaken departmentally by the enterprises themselves and if the period of construction has been long enough to lure the workers into hopes of permanent absorption.

(iii) Through inexperience and under political pressures, many public enterprises have tended to recruit at the very beginning of operations numbers that are indicated in the project documents as the full-operations contingent.[14] Thus the enterprise starts with surplus labour and it is unlikely that additional recruitment does not take place as the output expands within the installed capacity.

(iv) Finally, even where work studies clearly indicate the existence of surplus labour in terms of the prevalent or potential technologies, retrenchments are difficult to implement to the necessary degree and in desirable promptitude, in view of strong public resentment at the social costs involved.

It is possible that some elements of low productivity implying the excessiveness of labour prevail in certain private enterprises, the more so where trade union pressures on workload standards happen to encompass a whole sector or industry. But generally the causes of surplus labour mentioned above do not obtain in equal severity.

The empirical references that follow are intended to illustrate some of the points made in the preceding paragraphs.

References to surplus labour in public enterprises are available from the literature on Nigeria. The Development Corporations in the Western and Mid-Western States were 'plagued with the problem of redundant staff from the First Republic'. Their outputs did not expand but the wages and salaries bills 'more than doubled' during 1963-7.[15] The problem of overstaffing seems to have been a long-standing one; to cite one instance, the Elias Commission of Inquiry on the Nigerian Railway Corporation observed, in 1960, that 'The Union had alleged overstaffing at the officer level, whilst the Management alleged redundancy in the Junior service. We think that both were right'.[16]

There is evidence of surplus labour in certain public enterprises in Trinidad and Tobago. For instance, the Third Five Year Plan mentioned that 'a weeding out of surplus labour and staff' was 'required' in the Water and Sewerage Authority.[17] Likewise enquiries into the affairs of the state industrial corporations of Sri Lanka (in 1966) revealed that 'corporate managements universally complained of surplus workers, excessive absenteeism, and cumbersome expensive severance procedures'.[18]

A broad spectrum of illustrative data may be adduced from India.

The (Parliamentary) Committee on Public Undertakings (CPU) found a surplus employee content in the Indian Oil Corporation (IOC) at its Gauhati Refinery — mostly in the low grades — and referred to the difficulty experienced by the enterprise in retrenching it, 'because of opposition from the Union'.[19] The Committee cited staff figures in respect of the Burmah-Shell Refinery and the Esso Refinery, private enterprises at the time, with which the IOC's figures compared unfavourably, and commented on staff intake 'without consideration of any norm'.[20]

CPU's enquiries on Hindustan Shipyard Ltd are more revealing. With a strength of 5,507, the enterprise itself admitted that 'a medium-sized yard' comparable to theirs should not employ more than 2,000 men. The manpower utilization was about 38.6 per cent. The explanation provided by the enterprise is directly relevant to our discussion (see paragraph (iv)); the surplus was 'inevitable' 'owing to the labour policy of government and the social conditions in our country which have a bearing on the outlook of industrial labour'. The consultants' recommendation that 'the surplus labour should be got rid of' 'could not be implemented in view of the Government's labour policy', as stated by the Secretary of the Ministry of Transport in his evidence before CPU.[21]

CPU's enquiries relating to Hindustan Steel Ltd, one of the biggest public enterprises of India, showed that, as against the staff strength of 6,133 contemplated in the Rourkela project report, the actual number (in the departments covered by the project report) was 13,859 in 1964. The Committee discovered 'no efforts' to review the staff strength, despite the overstaffing admitted by both the Chairman of the enterprise and the Secretary of the Ministry concerned. 'It was proposed to utilise the surplus staff in the expansion programme'.[22]

In the course of its inquiries, in respect of Rural Electrification Corporation Ltd, as to whether the increase in staff strength was proportionate to the rate of growth of the work in the Corporation and whether any norms had been fixed for the staff, the Secretary of the Ministry stated that 'no particular norms had been fixed'.[23]

The maintenance of surplus labour has been obvious in the case of 'sick' textile mills, closed but taken over by the Government as 'relief undertakings'. Their labour complement was 'as high as 11–12 workers per 1,000 spindles as against the normal level of 5–6 workers'.[24]

Data on labour with a broadly similar purport are also available from the Audit Reports issued by the Comptroller and Auditor General of India. For instance, 'idle hours' were 10.3 per cent of total available hours, and 50 per cent of them resulted from 'want of material and work' in the case of Bharat Heavy Electricals Ltd.[25] Figures for Hindustan Zinc Ltd, as per consultants' examinations, also indicated a 'redeployable surplus' (of 112 out of the actual strength).[26] Similar surpluses were reported in respect of Neyveli Lignite Corporation Ltd.[27]

Surplus labour is not an exclusive problem of public enterprises in the developing countries, though it is much more severe and much less easily remediable. Let us look at the British Steel Corporation. Its productivity was comparatively low in the early seventies, by international comparison — say with Germany, France, USA and Japan[28] — and plans of modernization, which included the closure of uneconomic mills and aimed at doubling average labour productivity, were estimated to reduce manpower by about 50,000.[29] The origins of the problem may be unique but in essence it consists of a surplus of labour force *vis-à-vis* the right kind of technology and size that are needed for the viability of the Corporation under its market conditions; to quote from the 1973-4 annual report of the Corporation, 'a considerable degree of overmanning still exists at some plants'.[30] The problem has been gradually tackled. The total number of employees which stood at 196,900 in 1977-8 came down to 52,000 by 1986-7 — a reduction by 74 per cent (of which a small part owed to some recent privatizations) as against a reduction in liquid steel production by 33 per cent from 17.4 Mtonnes to 11.7 Mtonnes (British Steel *Report and Accounts 1986-7*, p. 41).

That rapid retrenchments are rendered difficult on what amount to distributional considerations is an interesting aspect of the present illustration. In the course of the evidence before the Select Committee on Nationalized Industries the Steel Committee observed, 'we are now faced with a situation where the Corporation says in its planning,"there must be wide-scale closures", at a time when the national unemployment figure is hovering dangerously near a million. You cannot expect people to respond to change in that sort of context, when really what they are being expected to do is to join the vast army of unemployed'.[31] And the Select Committee concluded that 'the Steel Committee, while fully accepting the need for the Corporation to maintain a competitive position and to install the most efficient plant, is able to countenance closures only where alternative work is available for those displaced'.[32]

The problem of surplus labour marks British Rail as well. Commenting on the 'stagnant' output per worker, Richard Pryke and John Dodgson estimated that British Rail 'could reduce its employment to 153,000 by 1981'. They went further to suggest that 'subsidization is the underlying explanation for the Board's failure to reduce its labour force'.[33] British Rail planned to reduce posts by 38,000 during 1981-5.[34] The total number of the Board employees fell by 21 per cent between 1982 and 1987 (from 212,722 to 166,989).[35]

To cite another instance: British Airways was estimated, in 1979, to have had '15,000 staff more than it should have if it is to run as efficiently as competitors like TWA, Laker and Britannia'.[36] The average staff in airline activities fell by 34 per cent between 1975 and 1984 (from 54,861 to 36,096); yet 42 per cent more of revenue passenger km and 34 per cent more of tonne km (freight) was handled.[37]

OECD Reports suggest that the problem of excessive wage costs in the public sector is common to several countries of Europe. For instance, in Spain there have been 'overmanning' and wage increases well above private sectors levels; and in Portugal wage costs in public enterprise rose faster than in the private sector and even in the administrative public sector during 1982–5.

It may be noted, in concluding these illustrations, that on the whole public enterprises in developing countries are in a more handicapped position in relieving themselves of surplus labour than those in the advanced or industrialized nations where alternative channels of employment are generally superior and a 'golden handshake' is, therefore, effective, and the emphasis on efficiency through productivity is relatively high.

Generous incentives

These are probably the least prominent, as a channel of distributional policies, among the four headings of employee incomes under consideration, despite their analytical relevance to the discussion.

Incentives are a legitimate cost item for an enterprise where (a) they aim at, and succeed in, achieving an output increment that the wage or salary emoluments themselves are inadequate to motivate and (b) they are linked to measurable enhancements in productivity. While this applies to public enterprises as much as it applies to private enterprises, experience shows that, in developing countries, the former tend to initiate incentive payments both prematurely and overgenerously. The explanation is as follows:

(i) For various reasons many public enterprises are underutilized and have remained so since inception. In such a circumstance low workloads tend to establish themselves, that is, at levels lower than those expected normally for the wage rates offered. Further, no scientific efforts are made to establish work norms; for the results might only offer a knowledge that, for social reasons, cannot be acted on, as seen in the preceding section. The view develops, and public enquiries support, that one way of expanding output is by introducing incentive schemes for workers starting from low work standards.

(ii) Where an enterprise has poor net revenues, it is unlikely that the workers can hope to augment their wage earnings with a sizable bonus (coming from profits) or even an appreciable quantum of indirect benefits through social services. In order to trigger their motivation, the management may be inclined to institute incentive schemes of a generous nature. The amounts involved will now rank as a cost item rather than as an appropriation of profit (that does not exist). The tendency for this to manifest itself is all the stronger in situations of monopoly power on the part of a public enterprise.

The emoluments gained by the employees in terms of the above description have strictly the character of being the product of a distributional policy. There is a tendency for the majority of incentive schemes implemented by public enterprises to be confined to 'worker personnel';[39] and this insulates them from violent criticism, for the distributional preferences of the nation are vaguely in favour of the workers. It is pertinent to note in this connection that many public enterprises, while being generous in the timing and content of incentive schemes, do not apply them to the managerial categories, especially at the higher levels. And if they apply, 'the bonus rates applicable to higher personnel' tend to be applied 'at gradually reduced rate'.[40]

Precise evidence is not easy to furnish in respect of incentives operating with the impact of distributional policies. However, that the phenomenon does exist is deducible from such information as follows. Incentive schemes are started at such low levels of production as 50 per cent of capacity, as against 'a reasonably normal level' of 75–90 per cent, as opined by P.K. Das. And they get started in the early stages of gestation itself. Their legitimacy as compensations for increased productivity has to be adjudged in the context of surplus labour and low workloads referred to in the preceding section. And as the higher levels of utilization are reached, the element of progressivity in the incentive rates is likely to be very expensive.

Further there is ample evidence of overtime payments to employees, even in a situation of surplus labour. To illustrate from Trinidad and Tobago, overtime payments accounted for 21 per cent of the basic wage bill in the Water and Sewerage Authority, 39 per cent in the Port, and 30 per cent in the Post Office; and the Minister of Finance questioned, in 1973: 'is there justification for [such] overtime payments?'[42]

Overtime payments in a situation of surplus labour have been a usual topic of comment in the reports of the Comptroller and Auditor General of India. The Bureau of Public Enterprises (in the Ministry of Industry) issued instructions towards the end of 1987, almost banning overtime payments. A saving of Rs900 crores is anticipated; this works out at about 16 per cent of the total employee bill in 1985–6.

Social expenditures

One of the most significant ways in which public enterprise policies proceed in the direction of national distributional preferences lies in their policies of 'social expenditures'. It is difficult to define exactly what these are and at what point on the scale such expenditures by public enterprises can be considered as exceeding similar expenditures on the part of private enterprises. Broadly these cover such items as housing, education, medicine, transport, entertainment, and holiday privileges. In respect of all or some of these many countries have laws that uniformly apply to private and public enterprises, but the latter in practice go beyond the legal minima under several heads. This is particularly true of enterprises located in remote areas where the development of townships and various incidental amenities seems to be desirable, if not necessary, and also of enterprises enjoying monopoly powers. The concept of public enterprise as a model employer gains prominence and any 'excessive expenditures' are condoned on the grounds of the social well-being of the employees, of whom the majority are believed to be in the lower income brackets.

Some of the most telling evidence on the instrumentality of social expenditures as a distributional channel through the medium of public enterprise can be derived from India. Table 2.3[43] relates to a large number of public enterprises of the Central Government, according to sectoral categories, and shows the significance of the 'social overheads' (the term used in the Report) in the context of their financial performance in 1974–5. They include township maintenance (less rents received), education, medical facilities, social and cultural activities, transport subsidy, etc.

Social overheads constituted an element of considerable importance in the incomes of the employees. They varied from sector to sector, the highest benefits having accrued in the steel and transport service sectors, where they amounted to about a seventh of the wage rewards. (If the services received by them were valued at market rates, the proportion would be higher.)

There are two aspects of the data that merit note at this point. First, the wage income figures are averages and refer to all employees. If the 'workers' or lower-income employee categories alone were considered, the 'social overheads' benefits accruing to them would constitute far higher proportions of the wage incomes of column 2. Second, if the data for individual enterprises, as against sectoral groups, are examined, both the relative importance of social expenditures as an employee income and their impact on the financial viability of the enterprises concerned are likely to be higher, in some cases, than what the sectoral aggregates reveal.

The incomes made available to the employees through social overheads constituted no small proportion of the gross profits of the enterprises (i.e. before interest charges on loan capital). Once again steel and transport services stood at the top; the proportion was about a third of the gross profit in the former case and a fourth in the latter, as can be seen from column 5.

Table 2.3 Social overheads of public enterprises (India) (1974–5)

Sector	Salaries and wages per employee (Rs)	Social overheads per employee (Rs)	Social overheads as percentage of salaries and wages (3) as % of (2)	Social overheads as percentage of gross profit	Gross profit after social overheads as percentage of capital employed	Gross profit before social overheads as percentage of capital employed
(1)	(2)	(3)	(4)	(5)	(6)	(7)
Steel	9,307	1,344	14.4	33.4	4.6	6.2
Minerals and metals	4,511	324	7.2	—	−5.4	−3.6
Petroleum	14,573	1,762	12.1	5.1	26.1	27.4
Chemicals and pharmaceuticals	8,875	1,084	12.2	20.7	6.0	7.3
Heavy engineering	10,474	1,122	10.7	12.6	11.4	12.8
Medium and light engineering	9,249	860	9.3	17.6	12.5	14.7
Transportation equipment	9,507	487	5.1	15.0	8.2	9.5
Consumer goods	6,701	411	6.1	15.8	6.5	7.5
Agro-based industries	4,135	—	—	1.0	35.5	35.9
Trading and marketing service	7,819			negligible	13.4	
Transport services	15,732	2,279	14.5	2.5	8.6	8.8
Contracts and construction services	4,289			6.7	6.0	
Industrial development and consultancy services	15,418				24.9	
Small industries development	7,910				1.9	
Tourist services	6,851				7.2	
Financial services	12,178				3.7	
Rehabilitation of sick industries	3,918					
Insurance	14,891				3.5	
Section 25 companies	9,890					
All enterprises	7,481				8.4	

Employee incomes

The impact of social overheads on the ratio of gross profit to capital employed may be gathered from a comparison between columns 6 and 7. The figures in the former column represent gross profit *after* social overheads and are obviously lower than those in the latter, which shows what the gross profit would have been if the social overheads had not been incurred. The differences between the two columns are not small in some sectors such as steel and minerals. The two figures are 4.6 and 6.2 for steel, the former being about 25 per cent lower than the latter.

Data for more recent years suggest that the social expenditure benefits have improved considerably. The Bureau of Public Enterprises claims that social expenditure 'more than doubled during the last five years', and that this 'indicates the significant role of the public enterprises in meeting their social obligations as model employers'.[44] The net total of social expenditure, after taking credit for rents collected, was Rs273.96 crores in 1981–2. Per worker (entitled to housing) it worked out at Rs2,179 on average. In some sectors the figure was far higher: for example, Rs3,511 in steel and Rs4,632 in chemicals. These figures are, in fact, in the nature of underestimates. For, the interest on the total capital outlay of Rs761.99 crores on townships was taken as Rs9.09 crores in the calculations. If a notional rate of interest of 10 per cent were assumed, the recomputed figures of benefit under the head of social expenditures would jump to Rs2,712 per worker on average; to Rs4,707 in steel; and to Rs6,109 in chemicals.

The trend of relatively high enhancements in wage emoluments as well as the socio-economic welfare cost benefits of employees in public enterprise in India continued unabated during 1981–6, as evidenced by the following data in table 2.4 on wages and the consumer price index numbers.

Table 2.4 Wage emoluments in public enterprise in India

Year (1)	Average annual per capita emoluments (2)	Socio-economic welfare cost per employee (3)	Consumer price index numbers (4)
1981–2	100	100	100
1982–3	112	133	108
1983–4	133	156	119
1984–5	151	197	129
1985–6	161	245	138

Basic data from Bureau of Public Enterprises (1987) *Public Enterprises Survey 1985–6*, New Delhi; and *Reserve Bank of India Bulletins*.

Distributional implications

The purpose of the preceding sections was to indicate the potentiality of public enterprise as a distributional instrumentality through its employee-incomes policies. The empirical material was intended to illustrate how it has manifested itself in some countries, though we cannot assert that every public enterprise in every country has adopted employee policies in the same manner. Nor can we assert that these policies have invariably been introduced by the enterprises as a deliberate distributional measure at their own discretion or even at the instance or under the direction of the government. Besides, we cannot be clear on the precise relationship between their policies and national distributional policies. It is interesting to note here that, in whatever way these policies may have developed, corrections on enterprise viability grounds are often difficult to introduce, even if there were no explicitly distributional reasons for the policies to start with. In other words, any alterations in them that seem to go against distributional ideas, however vague, are most difficult to introduce.

Before we go on to examine the distributional implications of the employee-incomes policies of public enterprises, it is useful to recognize a dissimilarity between wage levels and social expenditures on the one side, and surplus labour and generous incentives on the other. While all these are channels of placing increased incomes in the hands of the employees, the latter two place the enterprise in a situation of almost permanent disadvantage in terms of efficiency, for their physical norms of workloads and man-machine ratios tend to be lowered, perhaps never to be adequately rectified in an unemployment-ridden economy. The inefficiency can be infectious on the private sector as well in the course of time, the more so if public enterprises occupy a substantial place in the organized economic sectors, and if trade unionism is powerful. It is, therefore, desirable for the government to review the nature of the different modalities of distributional impacts with a view to discouraging in particular, the more disadvantageous ones. (The administrative implications of such a course of action are mentioned in chapter 7.)

Who benefits?

It is doubtless that the beneficiaries of the public enterprise policies so far referred to are the employees of the enterprises themselves; and in general the focus is on the lower-income brackets among the employees. In this sense the policies have a desirable distributional impact in so far as the employee population covered by public enterprises is concerned.

The question arises, from the national angle of distributional policies, as to how this looks in relation to the desirability of improving the incomes of the lowest-income brackets of the population as a whole and of restraining, if need be, the rates of growth in the income accruals of the less unfortunate sections. In most developing countries the employees in the organized or urban industry and allied activities, which most public enterprises cover, are not the major segment of labourers receiving the *lowest* wage rewards. The larger and really poorer sections belong to the traditional sectors and agriculture in particular, where those employed get relatively low wages, have seasonal or occasional employment, or are underemployed; and then there is possibly an army of unemployed as well.[45] Policies of public enterprises that add to the incomes of the relatively small numbers employed by them, however helpful in a partial sense, aggravate the conditions of dualism already present in the national economy. If national distributional policies are to be meaningful, this situation calls for public attention.

Some illustrative data may be produced from Pakistan. Real wages in large industries, which mainly represent public enterprises, have not only been high but have risen faster than those in the 'unorganized sectors of the economy'. (In 1983-4 they were about 185 per cent of the 1969-70 level.) The large industrial sector employs only 2 per cent of the labour force, while more than 50 per cent of it is engaged in the agricultural sector where the wages are low and employment seasonal. Real wages in the unorganized sector in the urban regions have also been low and declining since 1979-80.[46]

Dualistic conditions also develop as between public enterprises that implement the distributional impacts and private enterprises that cannot; and even as between public enterprises whose financial or other circumstances allow them to adopt significantly distributional policies and the others. For example, the Indian data cited in table 2.3 showed how the employees in certain sectors were better-off than those in others in receiving 'social overheads' incomes. In fact in a sector such as 'contracts and construction services' only two enterprises had noticeable 'social overheads', while the employees in the other enterprises in the same sector did not derive similar benefits.

The questions for public policy that arise are as follows. First, if public enterprises offer distributional benefits to their employees in some ways, can they, in any other ways, also benefit the other sections of society whose income conditions are equally poor, if not far poorer? This question will be examined to some extent in the next section. Second, if the government's budget were to be the major instrument in effecting distributional benefits to certain sections of the people, can public enterprises contribute to this process by making available a part of their surpluses to the public exchequer for general use? This question forms part of the discussion in the chapter on surpluses at a later stage of this study. Third, is it possible to syphon off certain obviously distributional activities of public enterprises (e.g. housing and medical services) into a general pool to be organized by the government — at a local or regional level — so as to cover (and benefit) a broader range of equally low-income sections of the people; and is it possible to expect from public enterprises a contribution towards the financing of such activities? An incidental merit of such a measure is that all enterprises, private and public, can be asked to foot the bill, on some formula possibly linked with their financial condition. Further, there can be economies of scale in the provision of the services concerned.

Who bears?

While there is clarity as regards who benefits under the employee-incomes policies of public enterprises, a great deal of imprecision surrounds the question as to who yields these benefits. In other words, who, if any, is adversely affected so as to enable the employees to enjoy distributional benefits.

Let us first assume that the enterprise is in the nature of a price-taker, that is, it does not control the price. The reason may be that imports come in, or that demand constraints make prices above a given level difficult, or that the government imposes a price control on the outputs concerned. As the distributional benefits accrue to the employees, any or some or all of the following effects are likely:

(i) The rewards to certain other inputs fall, or an increase in them is restrained; this applies particularly to managerial salaries.

(ii) Certain cost provisions (e.g. depreciation and maintenance) decline or are kept under check.

(iii) Research and development expenditures are affected.

(iv) The prospect of price reductions is affected. As a consequence, consumers who are denied price reductions lose opportunities of income benefits. Whether they deserve such a consequence, as compared with the workers whom they benefit, is a question that merits consideration on distributional grounds.

(v) In view of the additions to costs, reserve accumulations are affected and so are reinvestments, the more so if the enterprise faces serious problems in securing capital from external sources such as the government. Now the second order of effects of restrained investment unleashes itself. Possible additions to employment that the investments might have created are lost. Two further consequences may follow. Output expansions do not take place, affecting the consumption interests of the community in respect of the outputs concerned, and/or the prospect of any price reductions consequent on output expansions, so as to reach poorer demands than have been served, is damaged. On distributional grounds, therefore, the merits of the employees who derive benefits have to be weighed against those of the persons whose chances of potential employment or output availability or lower prices are affected.

(vi) The surpluses of the enterprises concerned diminish by the amounts of distributional cost commitments; if they already have deficits, the deficits are aggravated. The distributional implications of this circumstance will be discussed in the chapter on surpluses. But one point of asymmetry between public and private enterprises in this connection may be brought out at this stage. It is possible that increases in wage incomes at the expense of profits in the private sector have a welcome distributional effect, on the assumptions that profits go to the relatively high-income brackets and that shareholding is significantly skewed. On the other hand, as wage incomes rise at the expense of profits in the public sector,[47] it is the government (i.e. the taxpayer) that is adversely affected. If the affected beneficiary, either as a taxpayer or as a recipient of public expenditure benefits, is 'poor' on average when compared to the cross section of wage earners in public enterprise, the position is unwelcome from the distributional angle. Countries which have begun to emphasize distributional justice in their Plan strategy should bestow a sharp analytical look on this point.

Where the public enterprises are not constrained by the need to adhere to given prices, the sequence of consequences can be somewhat different. Prices are likely to rise, the more surely where government controls do not exist and the restraining impact of imports does not obtain. Even where the prices are subject to some degree of government control, the notion gradually develops in favour of price fixation on the 'cost-plus' principle; and what is important, additions to employee incomes will begin to be treated as an unquestioned component of the admissible costs for pricing purposes.[48] Likewise a case may build up for the manipulation of duties on imports, such that the local outputs do not suffer in competition from them for this particular reason. In other words, price reduction opportunities are under check.

Thus the interests of the consumers concerned are affected. In fact they may be the unique group that yields the distributional benefit to the workers, in this case.

It is possible that the price effect takes the shape, not of all prices rising, but of price discriminations. These, in their own way, introduce distributional inequities among consumer groups. On the face of it, however, the situation appears to be one of no adverse impacts on prices on the whole. Here the benefits are yielded by certain groups of consumers. The question should prompt itself: are they demonstrably poorer than the workers who derived the benefit?

Finally, where public enterprises operate in competition with private enterprises in a given industry, the consequences of high employee incomes as a distributional measure will, broadly, be parallel to those described under the price-taker situation. One possibility may be specially noted, however. If, over a period, the adverse effects on the viability of public enterprises are considered serious, in the sense that the government has to offer substantial subsidies continuously, the government may prefer to introduce a price formula that helps public enterprises cover their costs. Private enterprises also adopt the new prices. Now public enterprises, no doubt, do not show losses; but the profits of private enterprises in the industry rise beyond what they were. And this has its own distributional implications, depending on how their increased profits are disposed of.

In conclusion, we may refer to the institutional questions that the distributional channel of employee incomes raises. Since social expenditures by public enterprises represent a use of resources that their managers are not empowered, basically, to decide upon, the extent of the social benefits that may be built into the wages, incentives, and other benefits, as well as into the very aggregate size of the workforce, warrants public scrutiny. The scrutiny should be two-pronged: first, it should look at interenterprise relativities; second, it should address itself to the basic questions of distributional equity in the economy as a whole. The larger the size of public enterprise in the country, the more important the need for such a scrutiny.

An aspect of the employee-incomes channel that calls for positive action on the part of the government concerns the application of remedial measures in the case of surplus staff. It is common for retrenchments to be resented by the government; but it ought to go beyond such a negative posture, by actively participating in national measures for the retraining of the retrenched employees and their re-employment. These are beyond the sole capacity of individual enterprises themselves, though their co-operation is not only welcome but purposeful, as evidenced by the circumstances of the British Steel Corporation. For instance, it set up a wholly owned subsidiary, BSC (Industry) Ltd, 'to plan and coordinate all BSC action aimed at attracting new industry to BSC's plant closure areas ensuring that this action is closely integrated with the continuing efforts of Government, Regional Authorities, and Local Authorities to create new jobs in these areas'. 'In addition to the financial aids available from Government and EEC Institutions, BSC is prepared to consider joint ventures in the closure areas, should these be desired by firms interested in expansion in them'.[49] On the whole, the efforts at relieving the British Steel Corporation of 'overmanning' are national in nature, with the Corporation participating in them actively.

It would be interesting to add a brief comment, at this stage, on the response often emerging from governments to demands for wage increases in public enterprises: 'yes, if they can be contained within cost economies or own resources'; sometimes more explicitly '*and* if they do not occasion price rises'.

Are wage increases, in fact, so innocuous as they appear to be when these conditions are satisfied? Do they not have any distributional implications nevertheless?

First, assume that labour productivity improves and that the resultant cost economy is wholly absorbed in wage increases. If we also assume that the alternative was simply that there would be no such cost economy, it is true that wage earners benefit but no one else loses or yields them the benefit.

Second, assume that other factors may have also contributed to the cost economy reflected in the statistical index of labour productivity. Now total absorption of it in wage increases implies some diversion of benefits from other claimants, including consumers who have a right to demand that a part of the cost economies be passed on to them through price decreases.

Third, assume that the internal resources increase, not through cost economies, but because of fortuitous factors including a sudden rise in the demand curve. An increase in wages under this event implicitly raises questions concerning the distributional equity in the sharing of enterprise surpluses.

Fourth, assume that the productivity improvement and the resulting cost economy are larger than the wage increases. Now the consumers as well as the beneficiaries of the surplus can gain too. The net effect can be a spread of distributional benefits among the claimants.

In practice, the situation, fairly common in public enterprise, is one of low initial productivity or workloads. What appears to be an improvement in productivity achieved through wage increases may in fact be what the workers ought to have produced in terms of the initial wage itself. The basic cost structure stands inflated and already contains elements of distributional benefit in favour of the wage earners. It is on top of this that the above analysis rests.

To sum up the discussion on employee incomes as a distributional channel on the part of public enterprises:

(i) The extent of the distributional impact has to be quantified, even if approximately.

(ii) Considerations of its relative equity, among different groups of employees, and among employees, consumers, and others, have to be meticulously examined.

(iii) The long-term effects on enterprise efficiency have to be considered.

(iv) The role of public enterprise managers in implementing policies that innocently or deliberately contain distributional implications in favour of the employees has to be brought under a systematic public review.

(v) An appropriate institutional framework, involving some degree of public intervention, has to be developed, so as to keep the distributional channels as well as the sequence of their initial and further impacts within the precincts of national policies in the field of income distribution.

A specific input policy

Before we proceed to discuss output and pricing policies, it will be useful to refer to a specific input policy, which many public enterprises have been persuaded by governments to follow, namely, input interrelationships with 'ancillary' industrial units. This has implications of wage incomes. (Appendix 2.3 illustrates the big efforts being made in India in this field.) The idea is as follows. As far as possible, a public enterprise is to promote ancillaries which produce certain parts and tools or semi-finished materials required by it, instead of either producing them by itself or buying them in the open market from any other source. The underlying theme is that such a policy helps in creating labour-intensive units which, in most developing countries, have the good effect of providing incomes for the unemployed or the underemployed. In this sense there is a distributional implication. Let us look at it critically.

It is true that the benefit of wage incomes accrues to a group of workers that may not have had any income. But this might be at the expense of wage incomes in the public enterprise to which the ancillary is linked. Unless the ancillary workers are assumed to be poorer than the workers in the parent enterprise, we cannot attach distributional value to the ancillary strategy of the parent enterprise.

The strategy may have a positive distributional purport in the following circumstance. Assume that the labour content in the production function of the parent enterprise is lower than that in the ancillary, and/or that the addition of the outputs in question intensifies the substitution of capital for labour. The benefits of the activity for wage incomes in that enterprise would be a smaller proportion than would be probable in the ancillary. Now there is a net addition to wage incomes, the parent enterprise and the ancillary being taken together.

Let us examine who yields the benefit. The answer depends on the precise nature of the cost structures. First, assume that the cost of making the product available is the same in the two enterprises — the parent and the ancillary. The only probable effect is on the investors of capital in the parent enterprise, in case a smaller proportion of the cost structure goes to the rewarding of capital than before. On the assumption that the recipients of incomes from capital are probably in higher-income brackets than the wage earners, the ancillary strategy may be considered acceptable. Assume, next, that the ancillary's cost is lower than the parent's. This may sound strange, but could be true under two conditions: (a) Where the parent enterprise is uneconomically large, the ancillary strategy can bring in the benefits of economical disintegration. (b) Where the parent enterprise is inefficiently managed, irrespective of the size economies, the ancillary outputs escape the cost-adverse impacts of its management. Now neither the recipients of capital nor those of wages in the parent enterprise are at a disadvantage; nor are its consumers. In fact if the ancillary passes the benefit of lower cost to the parent, all these groups may benefit in some measure.

Let us turn to the more usual situation: the ancillary costs are higher, for various reasons, for instance uneconomical size, technology, and managerial ability.[50] Where the parent enterprise buys the products, its final cost structure goes up and any or all of the following effects ensue: prices go up; prices stay constant, but wages decline; prices and wages remain constant, but dividends go down; prices, wages, and dividends are unaffected, but profit retention suffers; the dent may be so serious that the enterprise ends up with a deficit.

In the first case the distributional benefit comes from the consumers; in the second, from the wage earners of the parent enterprise; in the third, from its investors; in the fourth, from the long-term interests of the enterprise (which may range over its consumers, workers, investors, and the government); and in the last case, from the taxpayer, if the deficit is made good by the public exchequer. These are the effects to be considered in the trade-off matrix of the distributional strategy.

There is yet another long-term effect of this distributional measure. If the cost impacts on the parent enterprise are severe sooner or later they culminate in higher prices on its end products. These constrain its demand and rate of growth in demand, the more materially the more elastic the demand in the range of output in question. The growth of the enterprise is impeded. As a consequence there will be a loss of benefits on the part of the potential consumers as well as wage earners and investors. Whether this is an acceptable trade-off for the initial distributional benefit of the ancillary strategy, ought to form part of the public policy considerations.

Appendix 2.1 Wages in Kenyan public enterprises: an illustrative note

The purpose of this note is to provide a broad idea of the wage structures prevalent in public enterprise in Kenya, as may be derived from

Public Enterprise and Income Distribution

published data (contained in the annual volumes of the *Statistical Abstract* and the *Economic Survey*). The exercise seems to be rewarding in that it provides a precise illustration of the point made in the text that public enterprises can offer 'high' wage rewards which, in their turn, have distributional implications. The nature of the high rewards and their distributional propriety will be examined in the course of the note.

The evidence

(a) The data on average wage earnings in the public and the private sectors since 1964 clearly indicate that the levels in public enterprise have been consistently higher all the time.

Table 2.5 Average wage earnings in Kenya (K£)

Year (1)	Public enterprise (2)	Private enterprise (3)
1964	3,585	2,508
1968	3,567	3,156
1972	4,115	3,774
1976	5,675	3,661
1980	7,198	6,120

From volumes of *Statistical Abstract*, 1973 and 1981, Nairobi.
The data for public enterprise consist of parastatals and enterprises with 'majority control by the public sector'.

The private sector average rose by 29 per cent from 1980 to 1983, while the public enterprise average rose by 33 per cent (on the basis of the data provided in the (1984) *Economic Survey*, p. 53).

The wage disparity between the two sectors may be summed up in the government's observation in 1984 that 'average wages remain higher in the public sector, with private sector being nearly 20 per cent below the public sector average in 1983'.[51] The overall averages have their limitations; but the purport is clear.

This finding is of significance, since the growth in wage employment has been at faster rates in the public enterprise sector than in private enterprise until recently. The distributional impacts in favour of public enterprise employees must, therefore, have been considerable. The following graph (figure 2.1) reflects the growth rates, sector-wise, on the part of public and private enterprises during 1972–80. (The equal growth line (with 45° angle) is inserted for facilitating quick impression on higher growth rates in public enterprise in every sector of activity.)

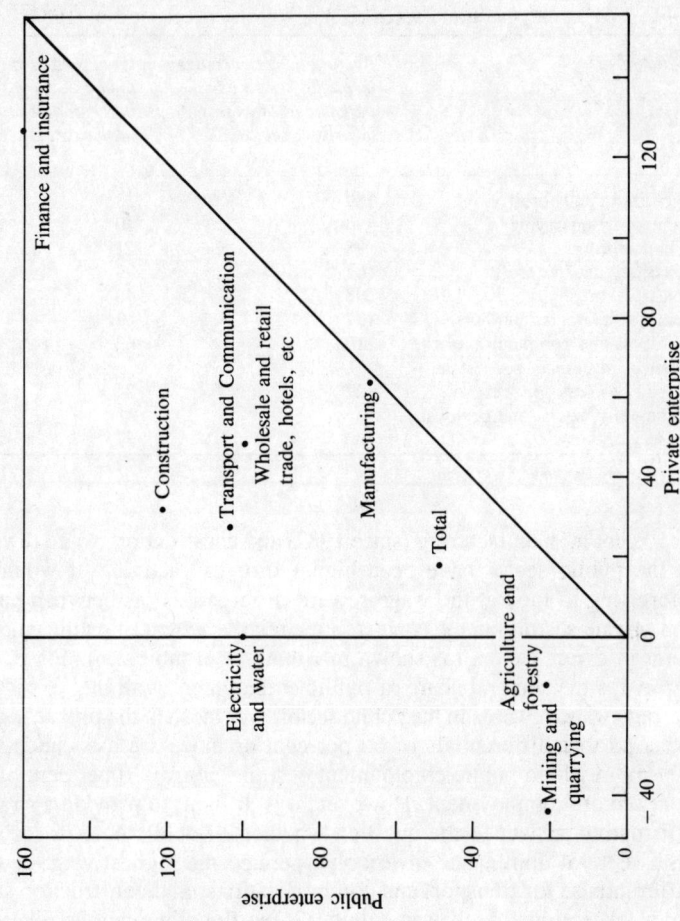

Figure 2.1 Rates of change in wage employment in public and private enterprise 1972–80 (%)

Public Enterprise and Income Distribution

(b) Wage rewards have not been uniformly high in all sectors of activity covered by public enterprise. This may be noted from column 2 of table 2.6, which indicates the level of average wage earnings in the public sector as a percentage of that in the private sector.

Table 2.6 Employment and wage earnings in the public sector (1983)

Sector of activity (1)	Average wage earnings in public sector as percentage of average in private sector (2)	Wage employment in public sector as percentage of total in the sector (3)
Agriculture and forestry	189	23
Mining and quarrying	456	40
Manufacturing	95	21
Electricity and water	107	99
Construction	98	48
Trade, restaurants, and hotels	127	7
Transport and communications	110	62
Finance, insurance, real estate, and business services	127	21
Community, social and personal services	160	77

From (1984) *Economic Survey*, ch. 4.

Except in manufacturing (since 1982) and construction, wage rewards in the public sector have been higher in every activity. It would be interesting to look at the wage-reward differentials (as between public and private sectors) in the context of the relative extent of public employment in given sectors (as shown in column 3 of table 2.6). Figure 2.2 compares the sectoral share of public employment with the 'excess' of average wage rewards in the public sector over those in the private sector. We find that differentials of 60 per cent or more are associated with sectors in which public employment occupies above 20 per cent of the total sectoral employment. However, it is difficult to provide a straight affirmative answer to the question whether all public enterprises with high sectoral dominance invariably operated the highest wage-reward differentials; for transport and communications, and construction stand out as exceptions. At the same time it is worth noting that the relatively non-dominant sectors of public enterprise (e.g. trade, restaurants, and hotels in particular) operated relatively low differentials in favour of their wage earners.

Another useful line is to find out how the aggregate employment in public enterprise is spread over sectors characterized by varying differentials in wage rewards, in excess of (or below) those in private

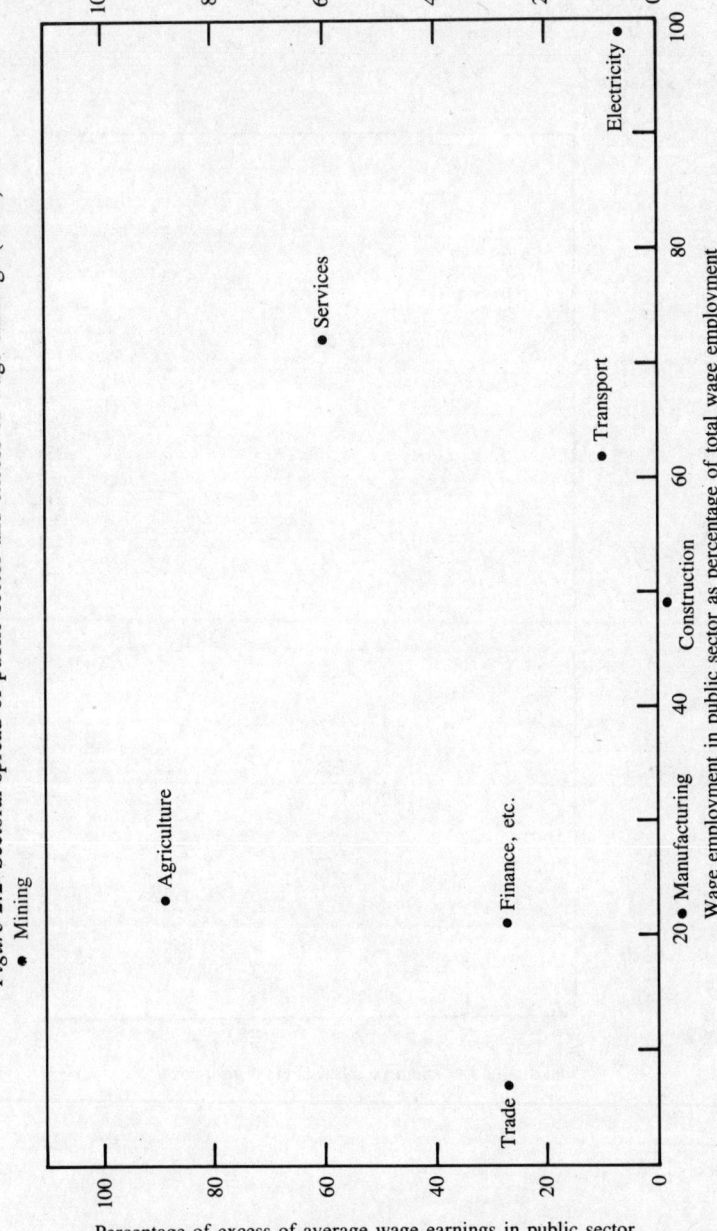

Figure 2.2 Sectoral spread of public sector and excess of wage earnings (1983)

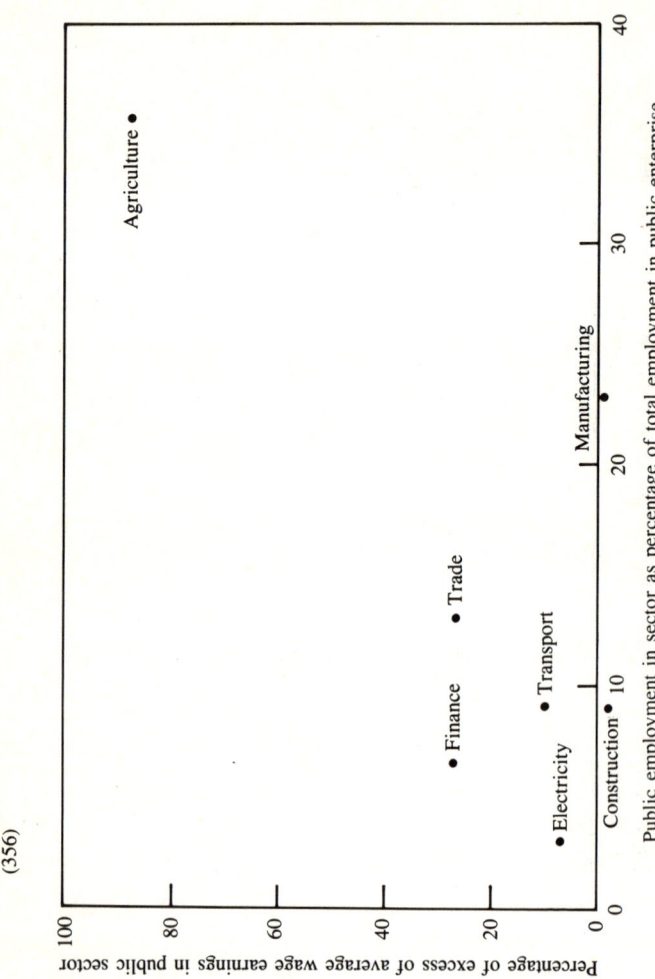

Figure 2.3 Sectoral spread of public enterprise employment and wage differentials (1983)

Figure 2.4 Employment and earnings in the public sector (1983)

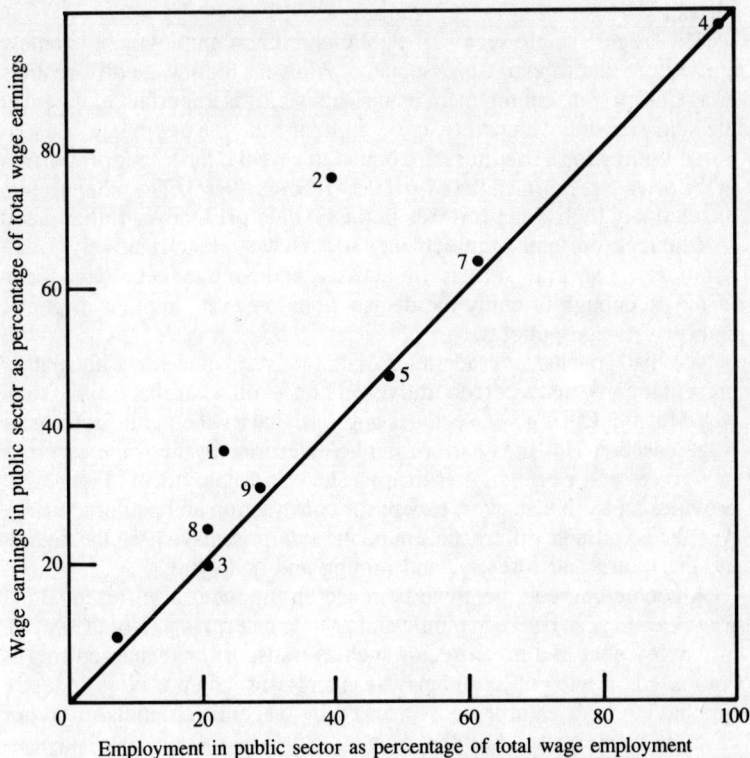

1, agriculture and forestry; 2, mining and quarrying; 3, manufacturing; 4, electricity and water; 5, construction; 6, trade, hotels, etc.; 7, transport and communications; 8, finance, insurance, etc.; 9, total.

enterprise. Are the highest differentials associated with large chunks of employment, and vice versa? Figure 2.3 is interesting in this respect.

The largest single sector of public enterprise employment, namely agriculture and forestry, is associated with very high wage differentials as against private employment in agriculture. (It is important to note that the statistics only refer to 'wage' employment. The aggregate occupational figures for agriculture are bound to reveal a far larger proportion in the private sector than the 64 per cent recorded here). The other sectors of relatively high wage rewards in public enterprise cover rather small percentages of total employment, so much so that relatively small numbers in several sectors of activity and employment have been fortunate enough to enjoy the distributional benefits implicit in public enterprise wage policies.

We shall conclude consideration of the statistical evidence with another presentation — just a corroborative version — on what share in the total wage earnings in a given sector is appropriated by the public enterprise wage earners. Has the share of public enterprise in the wage earnings in a given sector been higher than its share in employment? Figure 2.4 provides a positive answer, except for construction and manufacturing. And the favourable differentials in public enterprise have been the highest in agriculture and forestry, and mining and quarrying.

A concluding comment can be made on the sectoral differentials in wage earnings as between public and private enterprises. Not every line of employment in a given sector such as transport or manufacturing is composed of both public and private enterprises, and not every industry line having both enterprises is marked by wage differentials in favour of public enterprise; but the broad picture of differentials stays as described in the preceding passages.

(c) Interesting conclusions can be drawn on the scatter of public enterprise employment over different income brackets, as contrasted with that in private enterprise. The necessary basic data are available in Kenya. The following computations therefrom (table 2.7) are purposeful.

The following inferences are possible:

(i) The relative numbers below the Ksh400 income level are a very small percentage of the wage employment in public enterprise (7.3) as against a third in private enterprise.

(ii) While private employment is relatively far higher in the income brackets below Ksh700 (in fact three-fifths of the total occurs below that level), public enterprise employment is relatively higher in every income bracket above the Ksh700 level — most particularly in the medium ranges of Ksh700–1,500. Figure 2.5 clearly brings out these differences.

Table 2.7 Distribution of wage employment (numbers) (1982)

Income bracket (Ksh)	Percentage of total	
	'Other public sector'[1]	Private sector
(1)	(2)	(3)
under 215	0.7	4.6
215– 399	6.6	28.5
400– 699	21.0	27.9
700– 999	34.1	16.4
1,000–1,499	20.1	9.1
1,500–1,999	7.2	5.9
2,000–2,999	4.6	3.1
3,000 and over	5.6	4.5
Total	100	100

Compiled from (1983) *Statistical Abstract*, p. 251.
[1]Exclusive of 'central government'.

(iii) While differences in the skill content can be at the root of some wage differentials between the two sectors, the evidence is so overwhelming that significance has to be attached to the modal cluster of public enterprise employment in the Ksh700–999 bracket. The modal cluster in private enterprise employment is in the Ksh215–399 and Ksh400–699 income ranges — almost equally divided.

(iv) A small but interesting point may be added. While private sector employment almost remained stationary in its income scatter in 1981 and 1982, there was, in public enterprise, a steep fall in the figure for the Ksh400–699 income bracket, accompanied by a perceptible rise in the figures in the Ksh700–999 and Ksh1,000–1,499 income brackets from 1981 to 1982.

Appraisal

The evidence cited so far clearly suggests that wage earnings have been higher in the public enterprise sector in Kenya. Correspondingly income benefits accrued to the employees in this sector. How good can this be deemed from the macro angle?

Several points deflect the value of a positive answer. First, employment in public enterprise does not constitute a majority of wage employment in the country. It accounted for 29 per cent in 1982,[52] excluding employment in 'community, social, and personal services'. (This category comprises essentially government administration.)

Second, the poorest among the wage employees in Kenya are those engaged in agriculture and forestry. On the basis of the data contained in the *Statistical Abstract* for 1983 (p. 256) 64 per cent of wage

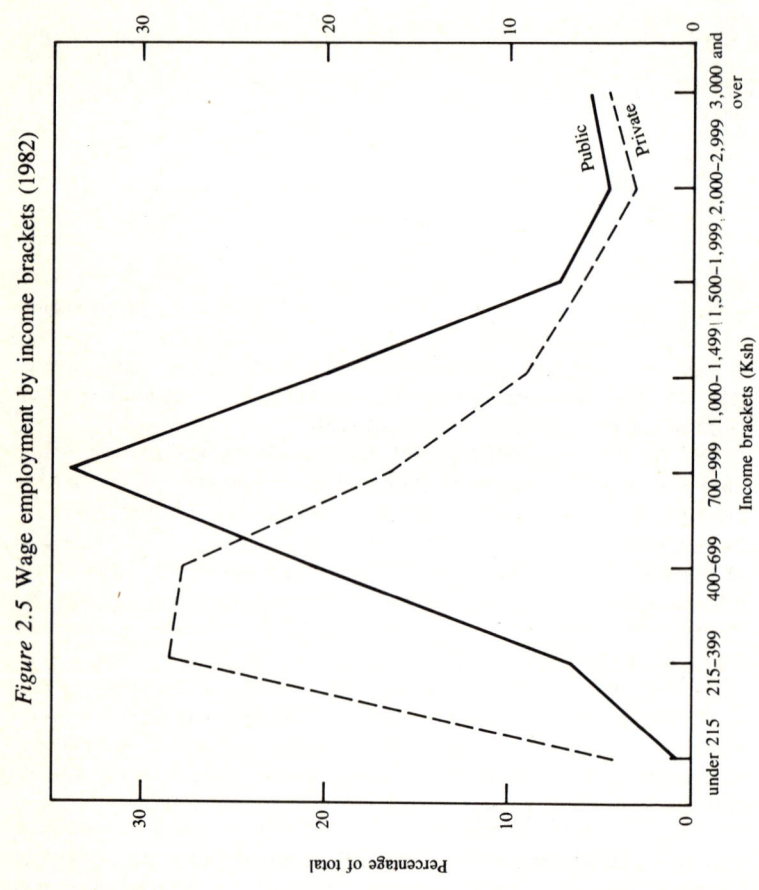

Figure 2.5 Wage employment by income brackets (1982)

employees in this line had incomes below Ksh400 in 1982, as against 11 per cent in manufacturing and 19 per cent in the aggregate. The overall modal value stands at about Ksh700, as against that for agriculture located in the Ksh215-399 income range. Public enterprise touches only some 25 per cent of the wage employees in agriculture. Though their wages contain distributional benefits of a high order (as evidenced earlier), the majority of agricultural wage employees fall outside such benefits.

Third, the rigours of dualism implicit in the distributional content of public enterprise wage policies are compounded by the fact that the population dependent on agriculture and allied occupations, whose average earnings would be lower than those of the wage employees enumerated in the official statistics, is extremely large. 84 per cent of the total population is rural and a major portion of that number is agricultural. The distributional benefits of public enterprise wage policies do not reach most people in that category.

Fourth, the available data do not allow us to draw inferences on the distributional implications for the different regions of the country. The issue is worth raising, however, in view of the glaring regional disparities prevalent in Kenya. For instance, Eastern, Western, and Nyanza Provinces have the lowest employment figures in terms of population,[53] the poorest *per capita* wage earnings are in Western, Nyanza, and Eastern Provinces;[54] Eastern, Nyanza, and Rift Valley are the top three Provinces with high percentages of the country's rural population; Nyanza, Rift Valley, and Central Provinces have for their modal range of wages incomes the Ksh400-699 bracket (while the other regions have higher modal ranges); and in fact Rift Valley and Nyanza have the largest percentages (of all Provinces) of wage employment in the under Ksh400 range.[55]

A meticulous survey of the regional aspects of the distributional benefits implicit in public enterprise wage policies can be rewarding. The inference is likely to be that the less developed regions are not touched significantly by these policies.

So far we were concerned with the question of how many — in particular, whether the poorest — have been within or outside the distributional benefits of public enterprises. Broadly many have not been covered by them — particularly the majority of the poorest. In fact these may have been under a distributional disadvantage, due to the phenomenon of losses almost continuously sustained by several major public enterprises in Kenya. Two recent observations by Finance Ministers may be cited to illustrate the financial condition of public enterprises:

(i) K£9.5 million was received by the government as interest in 1981-2 on an outstanding debt of K£417 million owed by public enterprises: 'a pathetic situation when one considers that Government is now required to pay between 12½ per cent and 15 per cent for funds borrowed on the local market, (*Budget Speech*, 14 June 1984).

(ii) 'Since independence Government has made investments, including guarantees to parastatals, of about K£900 million. During the same period, government has received only K£23.8 million in the form of dividends' (*Budget Speech*, June 1983).

Public enterprise deficits implied that the government has had to find alternative revenues to service the public debt (supporting public enterprise investments). This would imply tax enhancements. Clearly in recent years indirect tax receipts have been progressively larger than the direct tax receipts. The former were 197 per cent of the latter in 1979–80, but were 242 per cent in 1983–4.[56] Indirect taxes are, on the whole, regressive.

Thus the average taxpayer has been under increasing regressive burdens of taxation as a result of public enterprise deficits. In terms of the analysis contained in the text, the taxpayer has been yielding distributional benefits to the employees of public enterprises in Kenya.

Conclusion

This empirical analysis suggests a threefold conclusion:

(i) Public enterprise in Kenya has conferred significant income benefits to its employees.

(ii) The benefits have not reached a major segment of wage employees, nor many of the poorest, in the country.

(iii) A consequence of public enterprise finances has been a subtle but sure exposure of the public to regressive taxation.

A caveat in the end. This note is confined to the distributional implications of the wage policies of public enterprises. Distributional effects flow, besides, from their other input policies and pricing. Some of these might be favouring certain sections of people not favoured by, or adversely affected by, the wage policies themselves. (For instance, livestock farmers gain immensely from the income distributional angle from the loss-making Kenya Meat Commission's input policies;[57] so do a large mass of consumers of grains, from the pricing practices of the deficit-making National Cereals and Produce Board; and many agriculturists, from the relatively low charges that the loss-making National Irrigation Board makes in certain areas.) Such effects are outside the scope of this note but need to be appraised in the course of an evaluation of the totality of the distributional effects of public enterprise operations.

Appendix 2.2

Figure 2.6 Public enterprise (PE) proportions in employment and wage earnings in Peru (1974–9)

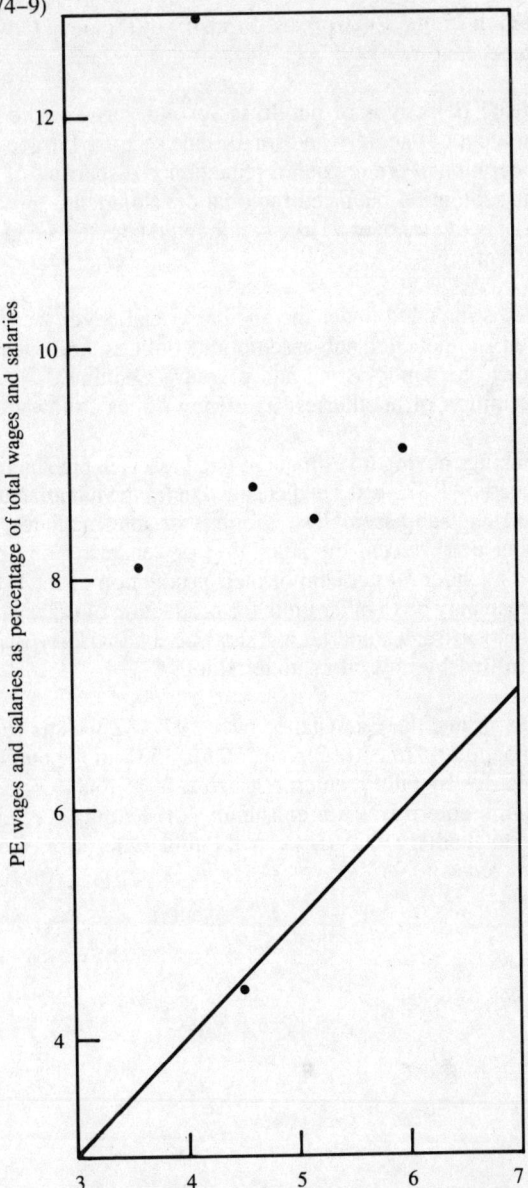

PE employment as percentage of all non-independent employment
(Each dot corresponds to a year.)

Appendix 2.3 Ancillaries assisted by public enterprises in India

The Bureau of Public Enterprises, Ministry of Finance, Government of India, claims that

> one of the objectives of public sector enterprises is to help in the development of ancillary and small-scale sectors. Larger social goals like generation of employment, reduction in disparities of income and wealth, promoting balanced regional development, and dispersal of industrial activities over a large sector could be achieved faster through ancillarization.

The activities included under the ancillary head cover the manufacture of parts and components, sub-assemblies, toolings, and even the servicing facilities like sandblasting and pressure cleaning.

The definition of ancillaries, as of now, is as follows:

> Undertakings having investment in fixed assets in plant and machinery not exceeding RS25 lakhs and engaged in (a) the manufacture of parts, components, sub-assemblies, toolings or intermediates; or (b) the rendering of services, the supplying or rendering or proposing to supply or render 50 per cent of their production or the total services as the case may be to other units for production of other articles; provided that no such undertaking shall be a subsidiary of, or owned or controlled by any other undertaking.

Progress in ancillary assistance over 1977–82 was as follows. The number of ancillary units rose from 550 to 1153 and the purchases made from ancillaries by public enterprises rose from Rs81 crores to Rs233 crores. Public enterprises are constantly 'off-loading' certain items of production to ancillary units (Bureau of Public Enterprises (1983) *Public Enterprises Survey 1981-2*, vol. 1, New Delhi, p. 226).

Chapter three

Pricing

General observations

We may preface the analysis of pricing as a 'distributional channel', that is, as an instrument in effecting changes in income distribution, with a few general observations.

(i) Appropriate price policies can be adopted by public enterprises, if required or permitted, in such a way as to base broadly their distributional impacts beyond the employee groups and touch low-income groups among their consumers. It is possible that, in some cases, the employees again benefit, in their capacity as consumers.

(ii) There may be situations in which the claims of consumers for 'distributional prices' (i.e. prices with distributional implications) and the claims of employees for 'distributional emoluments' (i.e. emoluments with distributional implications) are mutually conflicting. An obvious case is that of an enterprise whose revenue potentialities are limited, which has no access to any open-ended subvention from the government, and which is under stress to offer distributional prices to certain or all consumers. The more vigorously it adopts such prices, the less the room for adopting, simultaneously, distributional employee policies. In the course of time, however, employees are likely to exert their political strength in their favour in an attempt to reverse the position and succeed in most cases.

(iii) There is an interrelationship between pricing and surplus as distributional channels. Distributional prices that diminish the surplus raise questions of relativity as regards the merits of the consumers concerned and those of the potential beneficiaries of the surplus from the angle of income distribution. This point will be pursued in chapter 4.

(iv) Several distinctions under the term 'consumers' seem to be in order at this point. First, low prices may be offered to final, low-income consumers; and the distributional rationale as well as impact is direct in this case. Second, the low prices may be applicable, mainly if not exclusively, to outputs that are sold, not to individual or final consumers, but to enterprises which use them in further production processes. This is the case of intermediate goods. Third, an enterprise or a category of enterprise may offer outputs at low prices applicable to a whole sector, for example, fertilizer or agricultural finance. Here the distributional preference concerns a whole sector of consumption and is neutral to interconsumer equities. Fourth, an enterprise may offer low prices in a select region. Here the distributional preference applies to a whole region, as against other regions; and interconsumer choices within the region are not invariably intended.

(v) The concept of a low price or a distributional price needs annotation at this stage. In fact these two terms are not synonymous, for every low price is not necessarily a price motivated by distributional considerations. Used for the ease of expression, the term 'low price' in the present context connotes only that low price that is designed to serve a distributional end. This is sometimes accompanied by a high price in certain markets on distributional grounds in reverse.

Three aspects of the low price may be distinguished.

(i) The price may be lower than that of private enterprises offering a similar product. This must be an exceptional circumstance, limited to those cases where enforceable rules that confine the availability of the output to the target groups of consumers exist. The situation has characteristics of dual pricing. If the supply of the public enterprise output is smaller than the total demand for the output in question, the former has to be rationed in favour of the low-income consumers.

(ii) The price may be low in relation to the cost concerned, assuming that the latter can be established, even if approximately. It may be below cost, while the other prices are not; or the price may just equal the cost, while other prices exceed it; or the price may exceed the cost by a smaller ratio than the other prices. These are all different versions of the phenomenon of some prices being lower than others but not for reasons of cost differentials. Such price discriminations are not uncommon, even in the private sector, on the grounds of maximizing the net revenue. But there are two special points about low distributional prices: the prices can be lower than even the marginal cost[1]; and they may be available, not to any consumer, but to chosen groups of consumers on distributional grounds. Unlike a commercial pattern of discrimination, a distributional pattern of discrimination can entail even lower prices for given groups of consumers than they might be willing to pay, if deemed necessary on social grounds.

(iii) The preceding situation may be extended to cover a large multi-product enterprise which makes certain products available to consumers at relatively low prices, as against other products sold at higher cost-price differentials. While not uncommon in the private sector, this practice in public enterprise might be motivated, not merely or at all on grounds of profit maximization, but by distributional considerations. There is a large number of multi-product enterprises in the public sector in many parts of the world, and the category of holding companies, with or without legally distinct subsidiaries, is common in several countries — for example, Tanzania, Ghana, Uganda, Guyana, the Sudan, and Bangladesh. Such corporate structures make distributional pricing relatively easy.

The sequence of discussions in this chapter may be indicated at this point. We shall consider, first, prices of goods reaching the final consumers. Next we shall take up prices of intermediate goods and then follow with sections on pricing in respect of a whole sector of products or services and on pricing with an eye on regional development.

Prices for final consumers

Let us first discuss distributional prices for the low-income consumers of products sold directly to final consumers. A major problem in this case relates to the identification of the deserving consumers.

It is not easy, in most cases of portable goods, to know exactly who the customer or actual consumer is. The purchase of a soap, fabric, or loaf of bread can be made in any quantity by anyone that may not necessarily be the final consumer of it; and there is no system in vogue of the final consumer having to register his identity with the enterprise that sells the product.

It is, however, possible in certain lines of business to identify the consumer — for example, where some technological device exists, which is both necessary for the consumer to draw his supply through and helpful to the enterprise to locate the exact point of consumption. Electricity and gas are the most common examples of this category, though even here anomalies are not non-existent. For, a registered owner of, or contractor through, a given technological device may not necessarily be the only consumer accounting for the entire consumption in question. Subject to this, these enterprises are among those that can generally locate the consumer.

Likewise some enterprises selling services whose purchase is co-extensive with actual consumption can also locate the consumer. Transport enterprises illustrate this possibility. A railway can devise a system of cards of identification in respect of given categories of consumers, such as senior citizens and students, and, within the limits of enforcement, be reasonably certain that an intended consumer does in fact consume the service. Other examples include a theatre or a zoo which can ensure, through the identity card device at the box office or entrance, that the intended class of consumers actually consumes the output.

There can be other lines of business where the supply of a product or service can be made to conform, not to anonymous distribution, but to conditions of eligibility that can be so devised as to make resale of the product or service fairly difficult. A finance enterprise, for instance, can make sure that its loans reach a given customer and even a given purpose; so can a fertilizer enterprise, though with less certainty of non-resale, try to devise a system of sale to intended customers. A retail organization can locate some shops in 'poor' neighbourhoods (such as shanty towns) and sell goods at lower prices than elsewhere; here the benefit accrual to the local poor rests on the assumption that the costs of transferring the goods for resale or use in other locations offset the price advantage.

Such exceptions apart, not many enterprises find themselves in a position which enables them to locate the exact final consumer. Incidentally the devices of so doing may involve formalities that largely depend on government action or approval rather than on exclusive enterprise volition.

The more difficult problem is that of identifying the 'poor' or 'low-income' consumers. Obvious conceptual questions such as the following arise: do we go by the personal income of the consumer or do we take the income of the family to which they belong (and what exactly is the definition of the family in this case); are other circumstances than mere income to be taken into account in evaluating their merits as a poor consumer deserving a low price, for example, their or their family's expenditure requirements; what relevance has wealth or property, apart from income, to the identification; are factors such as the consumer's age or any disability (or any similar consideration relating to any member of his family) of relevance; is it necessary to look into such matters as the relative importance of the consumer's or their family's dependence on the product in question in the context of their or its total consumption basket — a consideration of no small importance where alternative products in a broad field of consumption like energy are of significance — and so on?

The questions enumerated above are difficult to answer in exact terms. Besides, these have to be answered, not by public enterprise managements, but by the government. The enterprises neither are geared towards such a task nor have the powers necessary to probe into the personal circumstances of the consumers implicit in arriving at the answers. This point may be illustrated by citing the evidence, on behalf of the Electricity Council (of the United Kingdom), before the Select Committee on Nationalized Industries:

> We are not qualified to look into social matters. We have no powers to enquire about people's income. It would be distasteful to us to start trying to apply means tests, and frankly our staff are not recruited for social purposes.[2]

Attempts on the part of the enterprises to identify consumers eligible for low prices are almost certain to raise interminable protests from those not included in the favoured category; and where public enterprises are statutorily forbidden from practising undue discrimination among customers,[3] such attempts are bound to raise serious legal complications.

Turning to the ways in which distributional prices may be made available to the poor consumers, we can broadly distinguish between two methods. The poor consumers may be identified and appropriate prices fixed on *their* intake of the output. Alternatively, the poor consumers are not identified, but price structures may be so evolved as to contain built-in elements of discrimination in favour of the poor or low-income consumers, serving whom might in fact be expensive. The latter have the semblance of a managerial technique of pricing as illustrated by certain electricity undertakings,[4] which follow progressive rate structures. (Such structures are not universal; in many cases the method of declining block rates has a regressive purport for the small and poor consumers.[5])

But it is not easy to deduce into a standardized consumption characteristic the intake of output by the poor consumers. Detailed statistical evidence recently examined in the United Kingdom suggested, with reference to electricity or gas, that 'small' consumers are not necessarily the poor consumers, nor is the converse necessarily accurate. So the enterprises cannot infallibly build into the price structures distributional benefits in favour of small sizes of consumption. In fact the Electricity Council thought 'that there were a significant number of relatively large users of electricity who were not well off'.[6]

A close study of a recent paper issued by the Department of Energy (of the British Government) indicates that tariffs for gas and electricity restructured in the interest of the poor consumer do not cover all the poor that deserve low prices; that they benefit indiscriminately some consumers that are not poor; and that they harm some poor consumers as well.[7] If these deficiencies were to be remedied, the enterprises would be called upon to introduce complex qualifications to the price structures; and whether the desired distributional goals are fully realized at the end of the exercise remains doubtful.

An incidental value judgement, that seems necessary, refers to the size of purchase on the part of a poor consumer that may be offered a low price. One may contend that his claims for favourable discrimination may be deemed to be at an end when he touches the limit of a 'merit' consumption, and that he has then to pay the normal price. If such were the premise to be built into the price structures, the enterprises face an additional complication in determining the cut-off point in respect of low-price consumption. Electricity consumption slabs for residential customers vary among the State Electricity Boards in India, illustrating that the cut-off points of 'merit' consumption are quite differently conceived by different enterprises. We do not know how appropriate the differences are in 'distributional' terms.

Let us look at the alternative method, namely, of picking the eligible consumer groups and offering them either a concessional supply of the product or even a free supply of it within limits. The major problems in this case are as follows. Strictly, the consumers have to be identified, not by the enterprises, but by the government or by a suitably empowered public authority; the extent of price concession has to be determined by authorities outside the enterprise; and the quantum of any free supply, if decided upon, has to be determined likewise. This is, however, a simpler method in one sense. It does not call upon the enterprise to evolve its price structures as if they were intended to apply automatically to any consumer that came within their differential scope; and it leaves unmasked both the fact that it has an open distributional motivation and the extent of financial advantage sought to be given to the identified eligibles.

We shall turn to the question: who bears the financial cost involved in implementing price concessions to poor or low-income consumers? The two distinct possibilities are (a) that the other consumers offer the price benefits and (b) that the government picks up the tab.

Cross-subsidizations

These have been quite common in several public enterprises, for example, Royal Nepal Airlines Corporation, British Telecom, and National Bus Company (in the UK). In fact the view has been expressed in some quarters that 'one of the prime aims of nationalization was to facilitate cross-subsidies from the more profitable services.'[8] The phenomenon is illustrated by British Telecom which

> generates its profit on long-distance routes and these profits are used to support the local ends which feed the main network . . . . This pricing structure produces marked differences in the rate of return on different services — for instance, 16.2 per cent in real terms on trunk calls and a negative return of 2.8 per cent on residential rentals.[9]

However, the method of cross-subsidizations invites the following objections.

First, it is not certain that all the consumers whose demands are so strong that they are willing to pay relatively high prices for a given output are necessarily well-to-do persons; or that the discriminations involved necessarily agree with national distributional policies.

Second, distributional price discriminations differ from the normal commercial discriminations implemented by enterprises in the interest of increasing the net revenue in that, for one thing, the latter prices rarely go below marginal cost and, for another, whatever is derived from the lower prices in excess of the marginal costs concerned turns out to be a contribution towards the pool of fixed costs that the enterprise has to recover on the whole or towards the financial target that the enterprise is expected to meet. Not to offer lower prices to the consumers concerned might have the effect of raising the prices for the other consumers to still higher levels.[10]

Third, if the higher prices within the system of cross-subsidizations apply to industry and business, there can be second-round effects in the sense that the prices of many products and services may rise and there might be adverse consequences for exports as well.[11]

Fourth, the generality of the consumers are likely to object to price discriminations that smack of cross-subsidizations, especially where they seem to emerge from no definitive instruction from the government. (Where the latter exists, presumably Parliament concerns itself with the equity of the measure.) Where strong consumer organizations are set up under the statute, this point cannot be overlooked.[12]

Government subsidy

This method of financing low distributional prices is preferable from several points of view. First, it places the burdens of social policy where they belong, namely, on the public budget. And this ensures that the costs involved duly come up for the necessary kind of scrutiny by parliamentary and other bodies concerned with government expenditures. The role of public enterprises will be rightly limited to being *channels* of convenience, while the rationale of, as well as the support for, the distributional prices comes from the government.

Second, it will be possible, if not implicitly necessary, for the government and the parliamentary agencies concerned to approach the question of subsidizing a given group of poor or low-income consumers as a question in its own right as distinct from the narrower issue of offering low prices in respect of a given product. All products that can be relevantly considered together (for example, not electricity only, but electricity, coal, and gas; not rail transport only, but roads, shipping, etc., as well) may be so considered; and a policy of subsidization of the merit consumptions of given groups of consumers in broad but related fields can be evolved. Individual enterprises can be left to pursue normal, commercial price structures; and any elements of social inequity, attributable to or implicit in them, can be picked up, to whichever enterprise or product they relate, for redressal through subsidy from the government budget.

Third, the policy of government subsidization relieves certain markets of the obligation to subsidize some consumers on distributional grounds and allows them to plan their intake of a given product at commercial prices with corresponding advantages in the pricing and marketing of their own products.

The question as to whether the amount required for offering the distributional subsidies is easy to find from the government budget is quite an independent one. (In the recent study *Energy Tariffs and the Poor* in the United Kingdom it was observed that 'an assured 50p a week to all those in the same social security categories could be provided without tariff adjustments if the Exchequer could make available sums of this order', though in the concluding paragraph it was suspected that 'any Government subvention would raise serious public expenditure difficulties'.[13] This is an important problem in practice. If the government finds it difficult to provide the necessary funds in its annual budget — under given ceilings of Ministry expenditure — either because the money is not there or because it is not easy to obtain Parliament's approval, the distributional aims underlying the proposal of subsidy can remain unimplemented.

Let us next consider the several ways in which government may implement the policy of subsidization.

One way would be to identify the deserving consumer and the nature and extent of his merit consumption and, while requiring the enterprise concerned to entitle him to a given price concession, offer the enterprise a reimbursement towards the concession. As an approximate example of the method, though not exactly of distributional motivation, may be cited the 'Public Service Obligation' (PSO) payments made by the British Government to the transport agencies in respect of losses identified as 'those attributable to individual services'. 'The purpose of payment is to benefit the user, not the transport operator'.[14] Similar are the payments made to public transport operators 'on behalf of certain users or user groups', for example schoolchildren with season tickets, travel by pensioners, and semi-disabled people. The payments by public authorities in such cases are 'so far as management is concerned, simply another type of fare payment.'[15]

A simple variation of the above method is that the government determines a lump-sum figure to cover the distributional price subsidies with reference to an enterprise and offers it at the end of the year. (In fact the PSO payments in the UK have tended to approximate to this method.) The main problem here is that, even if the figure corresponds, at the time of the original computation, to the aggregate of individual consumer or consumer-group eligibilities, the enterprise soon gets stuck to that figure or to a lower figure of subsidy as time passes. If the area of claims for such price concessions does not gradually contract or actually expands, the enterprise may find itself exposed to net revenue diminutions, other things being equal. Though it may argue for corresponding increases in the subsidy, it is likely to encounter difficulties inherent in the system of a lump-sum grant.

Two possibilities ensue. One is that the enterprise tends to work at a lower rate of surplus than may have been targeted in terms of internal financial discipline or external stipulation. The burdens of the distributional prices tend to be borne by those affected by reductions in the surplus — a point to be considered in chapter 4. The other is that the enterprise is impelled to maintain its rate of surplus, the more so if it is under the rigid stress of meeting a target of net revenue or of an external financial limit as fixed by the government. This tendency is all the more certain if the decline in net revenue places it in the red. Now it may try to tilt its price structures in such a way that the strong markets pay more than before. In other words, it operates interconsumer cross-subsidizations, the objections to which we have already noted.

There are not many examples of clear policy in favour of direct governmental subsidization of consumers identified as deserving low prices. One near example, cited already, comes from the UK practice of local authorities offering 'revenue support' and 'concessionary fares payments' to bus operators, so as to realize the social objectives, respectively, of availability of rural services and assistance to disabled and elderly people. These constituted, respectively, 28 per cent and 10 per cent of the gross resources of stage services operators in 1982–3.[16] Even in this example, it may be noted, the subsidies were not handed to the consumers but paid to the enterprises on some quantification of the consumer interests sought to be protected.

This section may be concluded with a citation from Bangladesh, which reflects an appreciation of the inherent nature of the problem on hand.[17]

> In the event that the state policy wants to protect certain sectors of society from high prices a conflict of objectives arises as between the goal of compelling enterprises to operate on commercial principles and an obligation to the consumers. Here it may be argued that regulating prices of the enterprises is not an efficient or necessarily just way of compensating consumers. This should be done if so desired *by budgetary subsidies and distributional controls*. Budgetary subsidies will enable the government to identify the difference between the economic cost paid to the producer and the lower cost paid by the consumer. The amount of subsidy will then have its own economic and political opportunity cost which the people's representatives can assess when they determine the need and extent of the subsidy.

In the event that subsidized goods are to be provided to consumers at below their market price then suitable distributional institutions will need to be established to ensure against black-marketing and promote equitable distribution of goods at controlled prices.

Prices of intermediate goods

Enterprises producing intermediate goods and services constitute a major segment of the public enterprise sectors in many mixed economies. They sell their outputs, not to end consumers, but to agencies that use them as inputs in their own production and marketing strategies.[18]

Here the major relevance of pricing from the distributional angle concerns the second- and subsequent-round effects. For instance, if basic drugs are sold by a public enterprise — such as Hindustan Antibiotics Ltd — to other enterprises, the distributional impacts of its pricing policy are to be derived from what happens at the stage of the latter enterprises. Where the second-level enterprises do not directly reach the consumer except through further downstream intermediary enterprises, further rounds of effects beyond the second become relevant to the analysis; but it will be difficult to identify the effects in sufficient precision.

The distributional results of low prices on the part of a public enterprise selling its products to an enterprise can only be assessed in terms of what effect this has on the latter's pricing policy. If it offers correspondingly low prices, that is, if it passes on the benefit of its 'low' input prices to its own consumers, the distributional impacts have to be evaluated in terms of the analysis contained in the preceding section, as applied to the consumers of the second-stage enterprise. If, on the other hand, it grabs the input price advantage and maintains its own prices without reference to it, it can enjoy high profits. Now the distributional impacts of the original low prices are a function of how these high profits are distributed. If these are distributed as dividends or bonus shares, the persons who really benefit are its shareholders, not its consumers. The question, therefore, shifts to the nature of the shareholding: is it equitably spread among the relatively low-income groups in the community, or is it otherwise? In the latter case, the more probable in many instances, the effect will be an intensification of the distributional skewness.

If it is desired that public enterprise prices which are deliberately kept low are to serve as a channel of national distributional policies, it is necessary for the government to adopt appropriate measures in the above situation. One of these is to promote enforceable contracts between the selling public enterprises and the buying enterprises to the effect that the element of concession in the latter's input prices derived from the former shall be passed on, substantially, to the final consumer.

The term *enforceable* is the crucial one in such an arrangement.

If there are difficulties in arriving at such an effective system of low final prices, the government may devise a scheme whereby the profits of the enterprise attributable to its input price advantage are syphoned off into the public exchequer, through appropriate tax measures, so that the government may take further decisions on how the money is to be used in the pursuit of its distributional preferences. Whether the final consumers concerned end up with any benefit or not, the inequity of unintended gains accruing to the investors of the 'buying enterprises' can be checked in this way.

There is another facet of the analysis. Does the enterprise securing the low-price advantage pass it on towards an addition to the wage incomes? If it does, the distributional implication is in favour of the wage earners as against the eventual consumers. Examples that come near to this phenomenon include small-scale industry development corporations which offer machines and tools on low-price terms, including hire-purchase, to small units. Here the major benefit is an assured or sizable wage income to the workers employed in those units. Where the units are in the nature of producer co-operatives, the result is even more certain. It seems possible to speculate that where the intermediate goods represent items of intermediate technology, rather than of high and capital-intensive technology, the pro-wage benefit is probable. In fact the low-price policy in this case encourages the employment potential in the user industries; perhaps this may have been the intention.

Yet another line of analysis is possible. Does the low-price policy of an intermediate-goods enterprise have the effect of reducing its surplus or the wage incomes of its employees? After identifying this, one has to review alongside it the actual distributional effects at the second round in order to infer the net distributional impact of the price policy. Several possibilities of combined effects exist.

A. *The selling enterprise*

1. Wages decline
2. Wages decline
3. Wages decline
4. Surplus declines
5. Surplus declines
6. Surplus declines
7. Wages decline and surplus declines, in varying proportions

B. *The buying enterprise*

1. Prices decline
2. Wages rise
3. Surplus rises
4. Prices decline
5. Wages rise
6. Surplus rises
7. Prices decline, wages rise, and surplus rises, in varying proportions

The comparison should proceed on the following lines. If A1 is anti-distributional, is B1 compensatorily pro-distributional? Or, are the consumers benefitting under B1 the more deserving, in terms of distributive justice, than the workers losing under A1? As for the second line, the question is whether the wage earners of B are more deserving or less deserving than the wage earners of A. Line three raises the question whether the *profit* receivers of B are more deserving of a distributional benefit than the wage earners of A. If B is a workers' co-operative, the situation is effectively similar to that of line two. The issue with line four is whether the consumers of B are more deserving of a distributional benefit than the profit receivers of A. And so on.

Two problems complicate the practical utility of these analyses. First, it is difficult to identify the results as neatly as the above typological process suggests. Second, it is not easy to compare the distributional merits of a given set of beneficiaries associated with the second enterprise, with those of a given set of yielders of benefit associated with the first enterprise. These complications are compounded if we need to extend the analysis to an indefinite number of rounds beyond the second.

It is perhaps in order to conclude this section with two suggestions. Where, with the best possible analysis, the second-round results do not appear to contain positively desirable distributional benefits or where they entail distributional benefits of a lower order than what have been lost at the level of the selling enterprise, governments would be well-advised to re-examine the merits of low-price policies on the part of an enterprise producing intermediate goods. It is not denied that certain 'growth' considerations justify them. But these have to be proved.

Where the right (or expected) kind of price (and/or wage) results at the second level are not forthcoming, governments may do well to encourage an intermediate-goods enterprise to extend itself into downstream operations, so that there will be no unintended anti-distributional leakage of benefits. (The assumption is that there are no countervailing diseconomies flowing from the expansion of the enterprise.) Such a development has been canvassed in the case of Hindustan Antibiotics Ltd in India; but its serious limitation has always consisted of a very inadequate marketing organization.[19]

Sectoral pricing

Low prices for a whole sector of goods or services reach either the end consumer or an intermediate consumer. Thus the preceding sections covered this question in its essence. This section offers a few additional points.

The rationale of low distributional prices for a whole sector rests on the assumption that the bulk of the consumers are in the relatively low-income brackets and that a blanket low level of prices serves the purpose of yielding them an income benefit. If, in practice, all the consumers are the deserving poor, if the product in question approximates to the

Pricing

'elemental' category, and if its low-price availability cannot be abused for the especial benefit of certain of the consumers in some way, the intention of low sectoral prices is realizable. But these conditions are not always satisfied; and the benefits of the low prices can be quite indiscriminate. The richer sections of the consumers who do not need the benefits derive them in the same way as the poorer sections. No doubt the latter value the benefits higher than the former, considering that their aggregate expendable incomes are relatively low.

An interesting example of how the relatively better-off sections of the community derive the benefits of low prices far more than 'the less favoured and essentially poorer sections' is provided by the Compania Exportadora e Importadora Mexicana SA and CONASUPO of Mexico.[20]

Similar is the situation in Pakistan where the low electricity tariffs of 29 pies per kWh and 21 pies per kWh respectively in Punjab and Sind, and NWFP and Baluchistan for tubewells go to the benefit of the richer landlords (owning more than 15 to 20 acres each). Some of them probably sell water to others at their own price.

The consequences of indiscriminate benefits may be limited in such fairly elemental cases as bread and (perhaps) water supply. But where the low prices refer to sectors of electricity, small industry, agriculture, or house building, there is the possibility of the richer sections gaining enormously by acquiring inputs for 'commercial' purposes and for enriching their incomes and properties.

At this point an observation on the inequity of low sectoral prices contained in a recent report of the Economic and Social Commission for Asia and the Pacific, with reference to subsidized agricultural inputs, may be cited: namely, that

> there is no equity justification for subsidizing the inputs in many countries because, under existing institutional arrangements, input subsidies benefit the relatively well-off farm population and hence lead to adverse distributive effects, while their abandonment may not affect agricultural output seriously.[21]

Let us turn to another interesting illustration of distributional inequities through low prices — provided by British Rail. Referring to the poor financial performance of British Rail, accompanied by subsidization by the Government, Richard Pryke and John Dodgson observed:

> One of the principal qualifications of a social service is presumably that its subsidization or free provision has a favourable effect on the distribution of income in the sense of making it more equal. If so, railways are a very bad candidate because expenditure on railways is

accounted for to a quite exceptional degree by the better-off members of the community.[22]

The popular notion on the subject is otherwise, as sharply evidenced by the observation of a member of the Select Committee on Nationalized Industries (in Britain): 'I would have thought that it was generally accepted that on the whole the lower income groups would tend to be the greatest public transport users'. Pryke and Dodgson agreed, but 'if one looks at buses and not at trains'. 'If one takes the proportion of personal expenditure on methods of transportation accounted for by the top 20 per cent, the highest proportion relates to rail services'.[23] And they added: 'season ticket expenditure is particularly concentrated in the hands of the top 20 per cent'.

From the data provided in the Consultation Document[24] correlating income groups with rail expenditure, the Select Committee observed that 'it would appear that members of higher-income households benefit disproportionately from public expenditure'.[25] Despite certain arguments countering the statistical basis of this finding, the Committee concluded: 'it is none the less true that the London and South Region does benefit disproportionately from Central Government public transport expenditure, about £16 per head of population in 1975 compared with £8 elsewhere in England and Wales.'

Several examples of low sectoral prices are available from developing countries:

> The average cost of supply of power to the agricultural sector was 71 paise per unit in 1986–7, while the average tariff was only about 21 paise per unit in India, as observed by the Energy Minister of India at a Seminar on the Finances of the State Electricity Boards.[26]

> The Guyana Marketing Corporation sells imported edible oils 'at prices below cost' and 'the Government subsidizes the operations'.[27]

> The Ghee Corporation of Pakistan Ltd sells oil far below the imported prices. The difference (recently as high as Rs250 per maund — between the imported price of Rs450 and the consumer price fixed at Rs250) is paid by the Government.

> Sierra Leone emphasized 'equity' as 'particularly important in the case of enterprises rendering essential public utility services such as road transport and . . . in the case of Sierra Leone Marketing Board'.[28]

> The National Cereals and Produce Board of Kenya makes cereals available to consumers at relatively low prices.

Pricing

Referring to the pricing policy of the Food Corporation of India, the Bureau of Public Enterprises, Ministry of Finance, observes that 'the issue prices for rice and wheat do not fully cover costs incurred on procurement, storage, and distribution, as issue prices are determined by the Government on various socio-economic considerations. The subsidy paid by the Government to the Food Corporation of India comprises reimbursement of the difference between the economic cost of different food grains to the Corporation and their issue price, and the cost of carrying the buffer stocks'. The amount of subsidy paid to the Corporation was Rs570 crores in 1978-9 and Rs600 crores in 1979-80. The subsidy was about a fifth of the value of turnover.[29]

The Utility Stores Corporation of Pakistan provides essential commodities at lower prices than those prevailing in the open market. The main object is 'to protect the real income of the consumers, particularly of the poorer sections of the society including fixed income groups and also to act as a price moderator and a deterrent to profiteering, hoarding, etc'. By 1982 it had an accumulated deficit of Rs75 million as compared with its equity capital of Rs90 million.[30]

It is interesting to note that in some cases an attempt is made to deal with the indiscriminateness of benefits in one of two ways: by providing for some identification of the deserving consumers or by permitting some kind of dual pricing, the lower prices being ensured to apply to the deserving consumers. The problems of identifying the deserving consumers and ensuring supply to them only have already been dealt with in the earlier sections. To single out an ethnic group, as in Malaysia,[31] or tribals or rural dwellers helps to some extent; but within such a large category of consumer beneficiaries the benefits can be indiscriminate.

An interesting example of the dual pricing technique comes from India, in the context of the 'public distribution system' which is assigned 'a major role in ensuring supplies of essential consumer goods of mass consumption to people at reasonable prices, particularly to the weaker sections of the community'.[32] The technique ultimately involves either an assured supply to everyone at low prices up to what is considered as a merit-consumption ceiling, leaving further consumption to market forces of pricing, or limiting the low-price supply to an identified 'mass' clientele.

Two concluding observations may be made. First, the merits of low sectoral prices are proportional to the enforceability of provisions against the indiscriminate leakages of distributional benefits among consumer groups. The modalities of enforcement may eventually consist of disaggregating the 'sector' into sub-markets, to one or some of which the low sectoral prices apply: for example, farmers with less than 5 acres, or potential houseowners with no prior house property or applicants for houses within x square feet of plinth area, or 'first-time' entrepreneurs applying for loans from an industrial estates corporation.

Second, some annotation of 'low' prices, further to what was provided in the earlier sections, is specially called for in the present context. How low the prices are is, partly, a function of what the recoverable costs are taken to be. If there are built-in cost reliefs in the capital structures of an enterprise expected to offer low sectoral prices (e.g. through low-interest loans or equity on which a dividend is not demanded by the government) its prices do not necessarily appear to be low since they appear to cover the costs. In reality, the economic costs are not covered and the prices are really low. Several public enterprises are offered such soft capital structures so as to enable them to work at low prices benefiting a whole sector of consumption.

We may conclude this section with an interesting illustration. The Housing and Urban Development Corporation Ltd in India operates as an instrument of distributional policies, as evidenced by the obvious differences in the rates of interest it charges on its loans to the different categories of borrowers. The lowest income brackets and backward sections get relatively low rates; for example,

EWS I category	5.0 per cent
EWS II	7.0
(both within a monthly income of up to Rs600)	
Low-income group I	8.5
Low-income group II	9.0
(both with a monthly income of Rs701–1,500)	
Middle-income group I	11.0
Middle-income group II	12.5
(both with a monthly income of Rs1,501–2,500)	
High-income group	13.5
(with a monthly income above Rs2,500)	

Further the EWS groups have a repayment period of 22 years as against 15 years in the other cases.

The accounts of the enterprise reveal a net profit of Rs13.4 crores; and one may gain the quick impression that the higher-interest-bearing customers are cross-subsidizing the others. The real fact is different, as an analysis of the capital costs of the enterprise bears out. The net profit figure results from an actual payment of some 8.0 per cent interest on the loan capital of Rs668 crores and no payment of any dividend or profit transfer on the share capital and reserves of Rs188 crores to the government. Taking the cost of the shareholder's equity at a notional rate of 10 per cent and adding some 4 per cent to the loan interest rate (fixed on old-time debentures) so as to bring it nearer to the market rates, the net return on total capital employed after providing for its economic cost comes to -Rs33.4 crores. This represents the unnoticed subsidy received from the government (or the taxpayer) and works out at 4.1 per cent of the total turnover (i.e. load advanced) of the enterprise. In other words, the borrowers, on an average, received this much of subsidy; and among them the spread of subsidy was clearly uneven, the lower-income borrowers enjoying most of the subsidy benefits.

This example illustrates several points made in the foregoing discussion. (The data are taken from the *Annual Report and Accounts* of the enterprise for 1986–7.)

Regional development policies

Let us turn to the distributional effects of public enterprise policies focused on regional development. The development of the less developed or backward regions has attracted the attention of governments all over the world. For example, the 1984–8 Plan of Kenya gives great attention to 'promoting a better balance of development among the various regions of the country';[33] and the 1980–5 Plan of India has for one of its objects 'a progressive reduction in regional inequalities in the pace of development and in the diffusion of technological benefits'.[34]

Among the strategies of development planning public enterprise investments and operations have been accorded a prominent place in many countries. Some of the well known public enterprises meant to undertake regional development functions are the Sudene of Brazil, Corporacion Venezelana de Guayana of Venezuela (CVG), Instituto Reconstruzione Industriale (IRI) of Italy (with its statutory obligation to locate at least a specified proportion of its investments in the underdeveloped south of Italy), and Damodar Valley Corporation of India (whose functions include the promotion of public health and the agricultural, industrial, economic, and general well-being in the Damodar Valley and its area of operation). Pakistan Industrial Development Corporation, to cite another example, has been marked by a strong regional development bias, as evidenced by the Experts Advisory Cell's observation that its units were 'wrongly geographically placed from the commercial angle . . . . The single major social objective was to provide employment for the local population'.[35] One of its units, Harnai Woolen Mills, was described as 'a classic case of industrial investment on the criterion of developing a backward region by providing employment to the people of that region'.[36] There is another interesting instance, from Pakistan, of a financial institution — Equity Participation Fund — specially designed for undertaking investments in small-scale industry in designated 'less-developed areas'.[37]

Broadly, the enterprises are of two kinds. They may be national in scope and coverage but implement 'soft' policies of discrimination in favour of selected regions; or they may be regional institutions focusing on the selected regions only. The distinction is material from the angle of who 'bears' the cost of their distributional policies. In the first case 'other' regions can be made to bear; while in the second there is no other region that can, and hence an extra-enterprise agency — the government, usually — yields the benefits. That is, the taxpayer does. While in the first category of enterprises the taxpayer may *also* pay, in the second he alone pays. Most probably, there is no other consumer group to yield a cross-subsidy.

Discriminations through pricing are possible in two ways. The more obvious one is where the enterprise offers lower prices in the chosen regions than in the other regions. Assuming that the costs are the same in both cases, here obtains a distributional benefit in favour of the former regions. A more subtle way is where the enterprise offers uniform prices in all regions, though the costs are higher in some of them. In this case distributional benefits do take place in favour of the latter regions. Several road transport and electricity corporations, serving geographically wide areas with quite diverse population densities, load factors, and average consumption characteristics, come within this description. For instance, the demand circumstances encountered by A.P. State Electricity Board in India vary considerably from one district (or region) to another within the large state of Andhra Pradesh with an area of 277,000 km^2 and a population of 54 millions: the *per capita* domestic consumption varies between 4.15 kWh in Adilabad district and 15.50 kWh in Krishna district (even overlooking the city district of Hyderabad with 53.11 kWh); and the proportion of agricultural to total low-tension load varies between 10 per cent in Vizianagaram and 74 per cent in Nalgonda (overlooking Hyderabad);[38] yet uniform tariffs prevail on electricity consumption throughout the state.[39]

The uniform tariffs applied by Water and Power Development Authority of Pakistan benefit regions like Baluchistan, where the costs of supply are high because of diesel generation.

The observation that low prices have favourable distributional effects within the region to which they apply has certain obvious qualifications. First, they benefit the consumers indiscriminately. Wherever possible, the richer sections can assume a lucrative entrepreneurial role, taking advantage of the low prices. They can even organize themselves as middle-men and resell the product or service concerned, earning sizable margins. Second, if the outputs are transportable, interregional transfers are effected by traders, so that the price benefits intended for a chosen region are spread out. At the minimum other regions, for which the benefits are not planned, also benefit. If adequate precautions regarding the product distribution do not exist, the very chance of the chosen region enjoying the price benefit depends on how much of the product stays in that region.

The regional income benefits flowing from a public enterprise are not limited to the price channel. More importantly, they flow from the fact that an investment has taken place and certain business operations have commenced in the region. It is even possible that the prices are neutral in their impact, the more so if the local consumers are not the major segment of its consumers at all.

The three direct media of income benefits, apart from prices, are: (i) the wage incomes; (ii) the input policies; and (iii) the surplus disposal policies.

(i) To the extent that the employment provided by the enterprise is a net addition to the volume of employment otherwise available in the region, the wage incomes have a real distributional benefit. In many cases the effect of the public enterprise investments is to provide a higher wage than might be probable in alternative local occupations; or to prevent the costs of migration on the part of certain unemployed or underemployed persons.

(ii) If the input requirements of the enterprise (e.g. raw materials, tools, repair and maintenance, and restaurant services) constitute a new demand in the region, activities develop to meet those requirements; and wage and other incomes accrue correspondingly. These are a secondary effect. As long as the secondary activities do not represent a bare substitution for some existing activities, in terms of numbers employed and/or wage and other incomes, the distributional benefits are real. It is improbable that the region, 'backward' by hypothesis, presents a 'bare substitution' condition.

(iii) If the enterprise raises a surplus, it is possible that a part of it at least may be used for reinvestments in the region, or for wage and bonus enhancements, or for contributions to local social purposes. These constitute a further channel of distributional benefits to the region.

However, the extent to which the region experiences income benefits depends on two factors, namely, the multiplier and the leakage. The higher the multiplier effect, the greater the opportunities for the emergence of incomes through secondary activities. This can be countered by the leakage factor.

Leakages can occur in favour of 'other' regions in several ways.

Except for the minimal inputs that have to be locally secured and organized — as in the case of restaurant services — considerable proportions may be obtained from other regions.[40] That is, the benefits of the secondary effects are effectively shifted to other regions. Even where increasing proportions of inputs are locally acquired and organized, the investments and the technical and managerial skills may (have to) be imported from other regions; and the benefits of surplus flow outwards correspondingly. There may also be heavy salary remittances outward. The weight of such leakage is the greater, the higher the capital intensity introduced into the production function of the activities concerned.[41]

At this point illustrative reference may be made to the results of an interesting analysis made of the textile project in the underdeveloped Baluchistan region of Pakistan: 'Despite being located in Baluchistan, the textile project is judged to have only a small direct impact on the province'.[42]

Two further questions remain for review. The first concerns the ethics of the distributional effects in favour of the chosen region. Even if we assume that they are, on the whole, more favourable to the low-income brackets than to the higher-income brackets within the region, what should be our conclusion on a national scale? If the income benefits have come out of some subsidization from outside the enterprise and the region the question arises: are the beneficiaries in the region more deserving than those in other regions? Political considerations are important here, no doubt. Apart from those, if the *per capita* incomes of the lower-income brackets are lower in this region than elsewhere and if the unemployment rates in this region are higher than elsewhere, the value of the income benefits offered by a public enterprise in this region is indeed substantial.[43] If, unfortunately, the leakage factor is powerful, it is the incomes in the other regions that tend to benefit in the name of public enterprise investments and operations in the chosen region in *its* ostensible interest. The other question is: who yields the income benefits to the region? Assume that the output is sold under conditions of competition and that, therefore, the enterprise is a price-taker. Assume, further, that the enterprise is exposed to some element of diseconomy through its location in the backward region. The loss that results from a relatively high cost structure and a given (lower) price is borne by the government as investor or as provider of a specifically voted subsidy for the enterprise. It is the taxpayer that yields the benefit.

If, on the other hand, the production takes place under conditions of monopoly, and if the price can be sufficiently raised to meet the implicit cost diseconomy, it is the consumers that bear the burden of the benefits yielded. The propriety of this becomes the more questionable, the higher the share of the selfsame region in the consumption. For, by hypothesis, the region is too underdeveloped to be exposed to the high prices. And the direct wage-income benefits in the region may be neutralized by the

Pricing

consumer burdens in the same region and by a curb on the multiplier factor in the case of sales to intermediate consumers.

These points are on the top of the basic problem of relative equity between the wage earners and the consumers concerned — an issue discussed in chapter 2, pp. 25–32.

Appendix 3.1 Cross-subsidizations in a monolithic enterprise: a case study

This is a note on the cross-subsidizations and the implicit shifts of benefit among the different consumer or traveller groups served by Andhra Pradesh Road Transport Corporation (the Corporation). This is a large public enterprise in India, in the State of Andhra Pradesh, serving an area of 270,000 km^2 and a population of 54 million. It has a virtual monopoly in stage carriage business, subject to the recent limited liberalization of entry by private operators on certain routes. (The data employed here refer to 1986–7.)

The Corporation is divided into seven regions, each with a workshop; and each region is divided into three to five divisions. Neither in fleet or bus kilometres nor in earnings are all regions uniform. The impacts of road condition also vary among them. The smallest region has 1,072 buses and the largest 1,652; and in terms of earnings the variations are between Rs33.9 crores (in Bhagyanagar region) and Rs83.0 crores (in Sathavahana region).

Earnings data are available not only for each route, division, and region, but for the different fare categories, for example, de luxe, semi-luxury, express, ordinary, city, and ghat services. The ordinary services are the most important, accounting for 62 per cent of the total earnings and 64 per cent of the total bus kilometres. The Bhagyanagar division, that is, the Hyderabad City, accounts for about an eighth of the total earnings as well as the bus kilometres.

There are wide differences among the earnings per bus kilometre in the different regions and divisions — between Rs389 in Ongole Division and Rs454 in Adilabad division (or between Rs394 in Krishnadevaraya region and Rs425 in Kakathiya region). In terms of earnings per bus per day the differences are even wider, for example, between Rs785 in Charminar (a city) division and Rs1,438 in Adilabad division.

There are differences in the earnings per bus kilometre among the different categories of services, for example, between Rs400 in the case of ordinary services and Rs443 in semi-luxury services (overlooking the figure of Rs573 in the case of the small segment of ghat services in one region, Tirupathi).

Let us look at the available cost data. These are disaggregated among the regions, fairly thoroughly. The extent of joint cost allocations is

Public Enterprise and Income Distribution

limited to some 10 per cent of the total costs. These are termed 'indirect costs', consisting of:

Traffic, Welfare, and General (Administration): allocated on the basis of workshop production of the units pertaining to each region;
Power, and licences and taxes: allocated on the basis of the kilometres operated in each region;
Depreciation: allocated (at 55 paise per km) on the basis of the kilometres operated in each region; and
Interest on capital and debt charges: allocated on the basis of the fleet strength in each region.

Equally meticulous cost disaggregations are not made among the twenty-six divisions, though there are approximate estimates of route-wise viability (entitled 'rate effectiveness').

There are no cost disaggregations among the different segments of the services (or product mix).

The nature of the fare structure is as follows. There is a difference in the fare base between the city and the mofussil (or non-city) services. The city fare, varying with distance, starts at 40 paise for the first 2 km and rises by 20 paise for every additional 2 km stage. The non-city fare starts at Rs1.00 for the first 5 km and rises to Rs1.10 up to 10 km and then by about 50 paise for every additional stage of 5 km. The kilometre fare base is otherwise uniform among the regions. Figure 3.1 shows the city fares and the mofussil fares. The former, it may be noted, work out lower.

Within the uniform fare structure, costs are not uniform from one region to another, as shown by table 3.1. The fare-cost differentials represent the internal cross-subsidizations, effected through — and made possible by — the monolithic structure of the enterprise. Column 8 provides one measure of the interregional shifts of benefit among consumer groups in terms of the margin between earnings and costs per km, expressed as a percentage of the average earnings in the region. The most glaring figure relates to the city services of Hyderabad (Bhagyanagar region), which suggests that commuters, on an average, derive a subsidy equivalent to a fourth of the fare they actually pay, from the rest of the consumer groups. That they receive such a large income benefit is one important finding of the analysis; that this is yielded by consumer groups (in other regions) whose *per capita* incomes are lower in most cases, is another; and that this situation directly results from the monolithic and monopoly organization of the industry, by and large, is yet another. The other region that is marginally cross-subsidized is Rajarajanarendra, whose (relatively high) *per capita* income status does not seem to offer any *prima facie* justification.

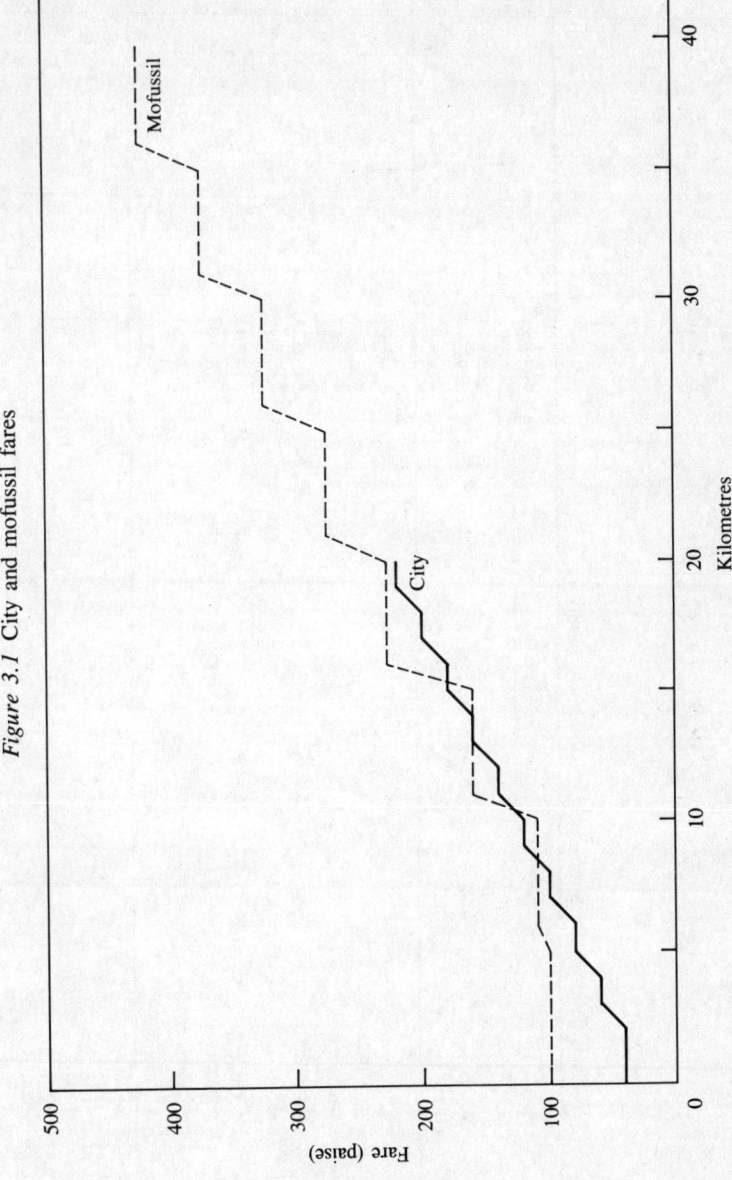

Figure 3.1 City and mofussil fares

Table 3.1 Classification of operations by profitability (1986–7)

Region (1)	Earning per km (direct + indirect) (2)	Cost per km (paise)			Net profit per km (paise) (1985–6) (6)	Crew utilization (km/day) (7)	Net profit as percentage of earnings per km (8)
		Indirect (3)	Direct (4)	Total (5)			
Corporation	420	366	42	408	(+)12	125	+ 2.9
I Bhagyanagar (Hyderabad city)	409	465	43	508	(−) 99	72	−24.2
II Golconda	427	353	41	394	(+) 33	126	+ 7.7
III Kakathiya	430	354	50	404	(+) 26	128	+ 6.0
IV Sathavahana	438	365	43	408	(+) 30	133	+ 6.8
V Krishnadevaraya	405	348	42	390	(+) 15	154	+ 3.7
VI Rajarajanarendra	411	371	42	413	(−) 2	122	− 0.5
VII Vikramasimha	408	350	35	385	(+) 23	144	+ 5.6

Pricing

If the cross-subsidizations were to be eliminated, the major device would consist of setting the fare levels differently in different regions, so as to pay due regard to the corresponding cost levels. (That the latter vary widely — and are the lowest in Vikramasimha and Krishadevaraya regions, on the significant ground, among others, of crew utilization — is clear from column 7.) But this would be difficult for several reasons: (a) a 'uniform' fare base is supposed to be 'fair'; (b) some problems of logistics, though not insuperable, present themselves in the context of many interregional and overlapping routes; and (c) the situation in the Hyderabad city services can prove to be quite complex. If the average fare level is raised sufficiently, there will be a big outcry from a vociferous commuter group. If the provision of services or the product- or route-mix is rationalized so as to bring the average cost within the average revenue, several route contractions will occur, triggering violent protests by the many affected route commuters. If neither a fare revision nor a product-mix rationalization is attempted, the deficit — and the commuter subsidy — will continue to exist; but an arrangement could be made so as to derive it directly from the government. This minimizes the need for the other regions to pay fare proceeds at their present high level. If, however, the uniform fare basis is not to be disturbed, there can be a case for improving the service or product mix and, in particular, to undertake route expansions at costs higher than the present average in the respective regions. The effect of all such measures would be to give the bus travellers in those regions the full benefit of a level and/or size of service that is appropriate to, and can be contained within, the fares which they are required to pay and which cannot be lowered.

If the Corporation were reorganized into a few units, each of them would work on a fare-cost formula that suits its demand and cost conditions. And there would be no (need for) interregional cross-subsidizations. A subsidy-deserving regional group of commuters would then look to the government for a direct subsidy in some way, in recognition of the fact that, when technological interrelationships do not inevitably interlink (regional) consumer groups, there is little justification for one group subsidizing another.

If the industry is fully deregulated, and entry and exit freely permitted, conditions of competition can so develop as to equate fare proceeds and costs (inclusive of a remuneration to capital and risk); and interconsumer subsidies do not persist on the scale that prevails today. An interesting contrast is provided by the organizational differences followed in the neighbouring state of Tamilnadu to which reference will be made towards the end of this note.

The regions are themselves very large with the effective fleet size varying between 1,652 in Satavahana region and 1,072 in Rajaraja narendra region (as against the 'viable' norm of about 600 held as a broad

Table 3.2 Some data on operations, division-wise (1986–7)

Region/Division		Vehicle utilization (km)	Earnings per km (Rs)	Earnings per bus/per day (Rs)	Occupation ratio (%)
(1)		(2)	(3)	(4)	(5)
(1)	Guntur	301	432	1299	88
(2)	Krishna	304	419	1274	81
(3)	Narasaraopet	302	417	1260	85
(4)	West Godavari	291	419	1217	84
I	Sathavahana	300	421	1264	83
(1)	East Godavari	285	403	1145	83
(2)	Vizianagaram	280	392	1099	70
(3)	Visakhapatnam City	262	405	1061	72
II	Rajarajanarendra	274	403	1104	77
(1)	Chittoor	324	395	1281	84
(2)	Ongole	314	389	1220	78
(3)	Tirupathi	304	442	1344	88
(4)	Nellore	302	340	1027	69
III	Vikramasimha	313	400	1251	79

(1)	Ananthapur	307	392	1204	77
(2)	Cuddapah	293	398	1166	80
(3)	Kurnool	320	391	1252	76
IV	Krishnadevaraya	307	394	1208	78
(1)	Adilabad	317	454	1438	85
(2)	Karimnagar	285	414	1179	77
(3)	Khammam	312	427	1331	77
(4)	Warangal	259	412	1065	77
(5)	Nizamabad	307	425	1305	78
V	Kakathiya	291	421	1224	77
(1)	Mahaboobnagar	308	415	1279	80
(2)	Medak	311	413	1284	77
(3)	Nalgonda	311	406	1263	78
(4)	Ranga Reddy	334	427	1427	79
VI	Golconda	317	416	1318	78
(1)	Charminar	199	394	785	60
(2)	Hyderabad City	196	399	780	61
(3)	Secunderabad City	208	396	826	60
VII	Bhagyanagar	201	397	800	60

guideline for an independent corporation in Tamilnadu). The 'interregional' level of analysis has, in fact, to be extended to the 'interdivisional' level, so that the price-cost relationships, division by division, can be of determinative significance in providing against interconsumer shifts of benefits traceable to no valid (technical) reason, other than the interdivisional organizational unification in the industry. Unfortunately we do not have divisional cost disaggregations, as meticulous as the regional disaggregations, though some physical indicators, shown in columns 2 and 5 of table 3.2, can serve as proxies to suggest that wide differences exist in the divisional cost figures and in the margins between them and the divisional earnings figures found in column 4. (It should not be overlooked that interdivisional cost (and even revenue) disaggregations are even more difficult than interregional disaggregations in the bus transport industry and that the figures, including the fare-cost relationships suggested by the disaggregations can only be taken as broadly indicative but not precise.)

It is the relationships between the earnings figures and the cost figures in the different divisions that reflect the extent of price (or fare) discriminations prevalent among them. While no definitive conclusions can be drawn, the data in table 3.3 making cross-comparisons between earnings (per km) and vehicle utilization (km per day) — an important determinant of the cost level — are of interest. All the highest earning divisions seem to be marked by the lowest cost conditions (of vehicle utilization), though the latter also characterize about half of the other divisions. The lowest earning divisions come under a wide spread of cost conditions; but some of them alone represent a combination of the lowest average earnings and the highest cost conditions (as suggested by the lowest vehicle utilization). These are the divisions, clearly, receiving a subsidy from the consumer (or traveller) groups of the first group of divisions and from some of the intermediate category of divisions as well.

The broad purport of cross-comparisons between earnings and occupation ratio — another cost indicator for which divisional data are available — is corroboratory (see table 3.2). The five regions with the lowest earnings and the lowest occupation ratios would be the 'subsidized' regions, while at least the six regions having a combination of the highest earnings and the highest occupation ratios would be the 'subsidizing' regions. (The identities of the regions are available in table 3.2.)

Cross-subsidies would be more obvious if we go by route-wise data. There are two very serious qualifications, however. For one thing, the 'route' is a fluid concept and there exist innumerable overlaps; for another, the proportion of what ought to be considered as 'joint costs' would be exceedingly high.

Table 3.3 Earnings and certain operational indicators

Earnings per km (Rs)	Vehicle utilization (km per day)				Total	Occupation ratio (%)		
	Below 250	250–299	300–309	310 and above		Below 70	70–79	80 and above
(1)	(2)	(3)	(4)	(5)	(6)	(7)	(8)	(9)
1. 420 and above	—	—	3	3	6	—	3	3
2. 400–419	—	5	3	2	10	—	5	5
3. 340–400	3	2	2	3	10	5	3	2
Total	3	7	8	8	26	5	11	10

The Corporation nevertheless produces estimates of 'route effectiveness' in terms of routes, buses, and bus km. Four categories of viability are distinguished: A, B, C, and D representing operations, routes, buses, or bus km, which, respectively, earn more than all costs, above 80 per cent but below 100 per cent of fixed costs, below 80 per cent of fixed costs, and not even direct costs. About 12 per cent of the 4,628 routes belong to the D category; in terms of bus km, a better indicator, the operations that did not even pay the direct costs account for about 8 per cent of the total operations and contribute about 6 per cent of all earnings. There are wide differences among regions in this respect. In the Bhagyanagar (i.e. Hyderabad City) region nearly half the services (or bus km) did not earn even the direct costs. The Vikramasimha region comes next, with about a sixth to a fifth of bus km — and higher percentages in terms of routes — in the D category. The A to D spread of bus km in the different regions is shown in table 3.4.

The D category of services has no commercial justification. And any social justification ought to be accompanied by a transparent public subsidy — from the state government or from the local authorities concerned, through a 'social contract'. As of now, the 'other' travellers subsidize them. It is difficult to compute the subsidy, since the extent of non-recovery of variable costs from the D category of services is not known. One thing is certain. They do not pay towards the fixed costs at all, which account for 10 per cent of all costs. The subsidy enjoyed by the D services is therefore higher than 10 per cent of the total attributable costs. (All the city services of the Bhagyanagar region top the list of subsidized services.)

As regards the B and C services, the conclusion for policy decisions are less simple. First, where a B/C service is integrally interlinked with an A service in terms of operations or as a traffic feeder, the joint performance of the routes concerned has to be evaluated instead of attempting to conclude on the precise viability of an individual B/C route. Second, the question needs review as to whether a given B/C service has just filled in a clear idle capacity or has drawn on vehicles and crew which have an opportunity cost that is higher than the revenue earned here. Probably this is the case, on the hypothesis that the aggregate demands for road passenger services place a heavy pressure on investments in buses for use where the cost-demand conditions are viable. To the extent that this assumption is realistic, the fare proceeds that fall below full costs contain elements of subsidy. These cannot be quantified since the extent of non-recovery of fixed costs is not clear, except that it is as high as 80 per cent and not below 20 per cent in the case of the C services. Locationally, the large proportions of the subsidized services (of C category) are in the Bhagyanagar (City), Vikramasimha, and Rajarajanarendra regions.

Table 3.4 Viability of operations

Region		% of bus km				Total
		A	B	C	D	
(1)		(2)	(3)	(4)	(5)	(6)
I	Sathavahana	77	13	8	2	100
II	Rajarajanarendra	57	19	19	5	100
III	Vikramasimha	46	21	22	11	100
IV	Krishnadevaraya	63	23	12	2	100
V	Kakathiya	79	12	8	1	100
VI	Golconda	76	15	8	1	100
VII	Bhagyanagar	3	7	42	48	100
	Corporation	67	16	13	4	100

A: Operations which earned more than full costs.
B: Operations which contributed more than 80 per cent but less than 100 per cent of fixed costs.
C: Operations which contributed less than 80 per cent of fixed costs.
D: Operations which did not earn enough to earn even direct costs.

On the whole, more than three-quarters of the services, in terms of bus km, are of the 'subsidizing' nature in the Kakathiya, Satavahana, and Golconda regions; in the Bhagyanagar (City) region the figure is as low as 3 per cent (see table 3.4).

For one interested in the identity of the divisional spread of the subsidizing A services, the clearly subsidized D services, and the most probably subsidized C services, table 3.5 is helpful.

The potential for cross-subsidization within a uniform fare structure, as practised by the Corporation, may be represented diagramatically as in figure 3.2.

Graph (a) represents A services which earn full costs or higher; graph (b), B services which earn at least 80 per cent of fixed costs but not full costs; graph (c), C services which earn less than 80 per cent of fixed costs; and graph (d), D services which do not earn the direct costs in full. AC represents the cost conditions in each case, D represents the demand conditions, and UF represents the uniform fare line. MC represents marginal costs in graph (d).

At the uniform fare F services in (a) earn a margin above full costs, which helps subsidize the shortfall of the fares below full costs in (b), (c), and (d). D is below AC right through in (b) and (c); and at any price or fare there is no prospect of recovering costs in full. If demand takes the shape of D_1 it is possible to operate so as to earn a margin over full costs if it is permissible to fix fares above the uniform fare level and if, correspondingly, reduced sizes of services are acceptable. Alternatively — and this would be the only option under an inviolable uniform fare principle — operations may be so rationalized as to make possible a lowering of the cost curve AC_1; if it can fall to AC_2 in (c) the element of cross-subsidy received by the services coming under the description of C services will be reduced but not eliminated. With regard to (d) the policy choices essentially border on whether to abandon the services that continue to earn below the direct costs in spite of all possible cost economics through service rationalizations. It is possible that there are some demands which are willing to pay higher than the direct costs; but they will be left unserved if a deviation from the uniform fare base is not acceptable and if the closure of services not earning direct costs is decided upon.

At this stage let us note the rationale of describing the fare-cost differentials as cross-subsidizations. First, no direct compensation is received by the Corporation from outside sources for its loss-making services. Second, the financial accounts as presented in the annual report of the Corporation indicate a 'net profit' of Rs7.08 crores. Apparently, therefore, the shortfalls in fare payments in certain divisions or regions are made good by the gainful fare revenues in certain others.

On a close look, the interest on capital, as charged in the accounts,

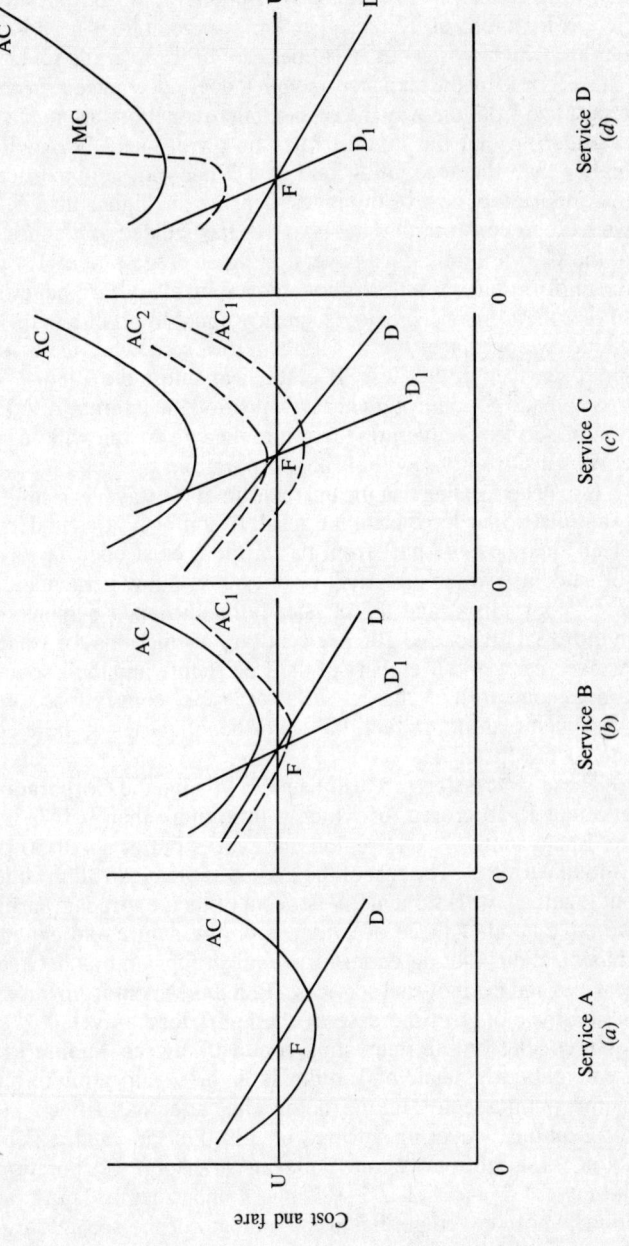

Figure 3.2 Viability under uniform fares

works out at 5.5 per cent of the figure of capital. If we recompute it at the 'economic' rate, roughly by doubling it, the Corporation's overall net profit figure of 12 paise per km changes into a net loss of 6 paise per km which works out at 1.4 per cent of the average revenue per km. This is borne by the taxpayer, though it does not come out from the annual report and from the way the accounting calculations are made. However, considering that the interest rates on government borrowings are far higher than the accounting rate of 5.5 per cent adopted here and that the opportunity cost of the investments is far higher than 5.5 per cent, we have to construe that the taxpayer has yielded an unnoticed subsidy to the Corporation's fare-payers, at the average rate of 1.4 per cent of the uniform fare. But this is not enjoyed by every fare-payer uniformly. In fact the D services enjoy a subsidy equal to no less than 10 per cent of the average fare; the C services, to a somewhat lesser extent; and the B services further less. If in the near future the 1986-7 'economic' loss is made good through high net profits, the internal A to D composition of services remaining the same, the conclusion will be one of total cross-subsidizations within the Corporation.

It may be recalled that the interconsumer (or traveller) shifts of benefits examined so far have been the result of uniform fares under conditions of unequal costs. Apart from these, there exist open fare concessions for students, which effectively work out as a low percentage of regular fares, journalists, and the physically handicapped persons and escorts in mofussil areas, and 100 per cent fare exemptions for students below twelve years, and Members of the Legislature and their spouses. These concessions are not analogous to 'off-peak' concessions, and have no 'cost' justification; in fact, the major beneficiaries of these concessions add to the 'peak'.

These concessions are estimated to involve the Corporation in a loss of about Rs20 crores, of which a little more than half is traceable to the Bhagyanagar (City) region and works out at about 30 per cent of its total earnings! The rest of the loss, attributable to all the other regions put together, works out at 2.7 per cent of their aggregate earnings. Here we have another piece of evidence on the nature and extent of cross-subsidizations among certain traveller groups and as between the city services and the mofussil services. (Reimbursement from the government is nominal, only in the case of the legislators' travel.)

In conclusion, an interesting contrast between Andhra Pradesh and the neighbouring state of Tamilnadu in the organization of bus services in the public sector merits note. The latter has fifteen independent corporations, covering an area of 130,058 km^2 and a population of about 48.4 million. While Pallavan Transport Corporation, serving the city of Madras, has 2,107 buses and Cheran Transport Corporation, whose coverage includes Coimbatore, the second largest city in

Table 3.5 Divisional spread of subsidizing and subsidized services

I 'D' services (clearly subsidized)

Nil	Guntar, Narasaraopet, Srikakulam, Chittoor, Khammam, Nizamabad
Below 5%	Krishna, West Godavari, Visakhapatnam (C), Ananthapur, Cuddapah, Kurnool, Adilabad
5–9%	East Godavari, Vizayanagaram, Tirupathi
10–20%	Nellore, Ongole
40–65%	Charminar, Hyderabad (C), Secunderabad (C)

II 'C' services (fairly subsidized)

Nil	Srikakulam
Below 5%	Guntur, Adilabad
5–9%	Narasaraopet, Kurnool, Khamman, Nizamabad, Medak, Nalgonda, Ranga Reddy
10–19%	Krishna, West Godavari, East Godavari, Visakhapatnam, Chittoor, Tirupathi, Anantapur, Cuddapah, Karimnagar, Warangal, Mahaboonagar
20–29%	Vizayanagaram, Nellore, Charminar
30% and above	Visakhapatnam (D), Ongole, Hyderabad (C), Secunderabad (C)

III 'A' services (subsidizing)

Below 10%	Charminar, Secunderabad (C)
20–49%	Visakhapatnam (D), Nellore, Ongole
50–74%	West Godavari, Vizayanagaram, Visakhapatnam (C), Chittoor, Tirupati, Anantapur, Cuddapah, Kurnool, Karimnagar, Warangal, Mahaboobnagar, Medak, Nalgonda
75% and above	Guntur, Adilabad, Khammam, Nizamabad, Medak, Ranga Reddy

Note: C – city services; D – district services.

Public Enterprise and Income Distribution

Tamilnadu, has 1,217 buses, the other corporations have smaller fleet sizes ranging between 368 and 841. Their finances are not interlinked, unlike those of the divisions and regions of the Andhra Pradesh Road Transport Corporation and there are, therefore, no shifts of benefits from one corporation area (or consumers) to another. Any eventual impacts of a losing corporation devolve on the government budget through the non-payment of dividends on capital or of a cess or additional surcharge on motor vehicle taxes. Likewise, the benefits of high-paying regions reach the government. It is the non-monolithic organizational device adopted in Tamilnadu that minimizes interregional cross-subsidizations. And under the uniform fare principle, the benefits of the high-fare proceeds in the profit-making regions reach the government or can stimulate service improvements in the respective regions; whereas the financial problems of the loss-making regions get shifted to the government budget in one way or another.

Chapter four

Deficits and Surpluses

The nature of deficits

Deficits and surpluses are the end results of the operations of an enterprise. Two of the major influences on their level, namely wage payments and prices, have been discussed in chapters 2 and 3. Brief references to the consequence of deficits as a sequel to distributional policies regarding inputs and prices have already been made at several points. However, there are two reasons why a separate chapter is necessary on the distributional implications of deficits and surpluses.

(i) Not all deficits are the consequence of distributional policies. (Other reasons consist of enterprise inefficiency and fluctuations, including structural changes and faulty investment decisions.) Yet any deficit, however caused, can have distributional implications. This point merits coverage in our study, since many public enterprises have been making deficits, even if they did not implement any deliberate input and output policies with distributional motivation.

(ii) More importantly, this would be the place for discussing the thematic question: who bears the cost of the deficits? It may be recalled that earlier references to the occurrence of deficits did not extend to this question.

It would be purposeful, in the prefatory stage of our discussion, to re-emphasize the point that the figure of deficit or surplus appearing in the accounts of an enterprise is not conceptually accurate in many cases. For, several practices of cost understatement exist. Not costing the input of equity capital is an obvious channel; moratorium on, or freedom from, interest on loan capital is another;[1] relatively low rates of interest are one other version; to treat reserves employed in business as a costless resource is yet another; tax exemptions are offered as well, in some cases; and so on.

The problem of deficit understatement (or surplus overstatement) is serious in the public enterprise sector.[2] This point calls for meticulous attention as we analyze the consequences of deficits from the distributional angle. We should not assume that they are limited to the apparent figure of deficits and that the public exchequer takes budget measures to meet the problems caused by *that* deficit. There are other aspects of budget response to the disguised elements of deficits, on the basis of economic costs of enterprise operations.

The effects

There are, broadly, two ways of dealing with the problem of deficits; and the eventual distributional impacts vary, accordingly.

One way is for the enterprise itself to find ameliorative solutions. Several possibilities exist.

> (i) If the enterprise has reserves, it may draw on them to the extent of wiping out the deficits. Apparently a simple way out, this works itself out eventually by curtailing the production activity and the output, and/or by affecting the investment expenditures, according as the reserves under drain are expected to have supported current production or investment. If these measures involve an adverse impact on the net revenues of the enterprise, the position gets worse. Further, underlying these results there may be a loss of benefits to employees and consumers if the cuts in output signify any restraints in the policies of employee remuneration and price reduction. The distributional implications of these results need to be recognized. Besides, it will be necessary to evaluate them by comparing them with any distributional motivations that have been at the root of the deficits in the first place. Does the final position amount to a reversal of the initial one, or do the employees retain their benefits while the consumers are now made to bear the brunt of the deficit-solving measures, or vice versa? Where the deficits have not arisen from any intended distributional motivations, the evaluation would proceed independently of such a comparison.
>
> (ii) Where the enterprise has no reserve to draw upon, it may effect cuts in working capital or embark on borrowings. The former leads to output cuts — a problem already raised; and the latter adds to costs and possibly to deficits.
>
> (iii) The enterprise may go all out for improving productivity, making sure that the costs of achieving this are lower than the results. The distributional implications of productivity improvements have already been mentioned towards the end of chapter 2.
>
> (iv) The enterprise may practise any helpful cross-subsidizations, if public controls do not stand in the way. These clearly entail distributional effects among consumer groups, as discussed in chapter 3.

The most important way of dealing with the problem of deficits is for the government (or some other public agency) to subsidize the enterprise.

Deficits and surpluses

In order to be able to do this, the government may adopt any of the following measures.

(i) Additional tax measures may be introduced. Two lines of evaluation will now be necessary. First, the distributional implications of the additional taxes have to be identified. If these are in the form of (progressive) direct taxes, they probably affect the higher-income brackets relatively substantially. Assuming that this is considered a distributionally acceptable development, the government's response may be considered as satisfactory. If, on the other hand, the additions to revenues accrue from indirect taxes, the likelihood is that they have regressive effects, the exception being the case of taxes on luxury goods. Now the government's response to the deficit problem is distributionally unsatisfactory. We have to superimpose on this another line of evaluation. If the deficits were caused by any deliberate pattern of distributional motivations, how do the end results — through the tax response — compare with those motivations? Are the tax measures justified by the distributional policies operated by the enterprise? Or, are the bearers of the additional tax burdens less well-off than the receivers of the distributional benefits from the enterprise? For instance, that would be the case where the benefits of a low price are enjoyed by a cross section of wealthy intermediate consumers, whereas the additional taxes are clearly of the regressive type.

(ii) Assume that the government prefers to readjust its expenditure plans, instead of raising extra tax revenues, so that some heads of expenditure that might have been undertaken, will be given up. In this way resources may be conserved for meeting the enterprise deficits. In evaluating the distributional implications of such a measure, we have to identify the nature of benefits lost by certain sections of people because of cuts in government expenditures and compare it with the nature of distributional benefits that the enterprise deficits initially harboured. If the latter are considered as superior, the net outcome may be treated as satisfactory. Or else, the distributional effects of the retrenchments in government expenditures are worse than those of the enterprise policies leading to deficits. This conclusion is the more probable if social expenditures (e.g. on education, health, and housing) are the first to be vulnerable to retrenchment choices on the part of the government.

(iii) If the government adopts the method of deficit financing in order to meet the impacts of enterprise deficits on its budget, it tends to fan inflation. The groups of people most affected by growing inflation are the fixed-income groups — in particular, the salaried middle class whose increased costs of living are, often, less completely neutralized through salary increases than in the case of the workers.

Though the inflationary conditions weaken the initial benefits of those to whom the distributional policies of the enterprise applied, it is others that may be more adversely affected. The relative merits of the two groups affected call for an evaluation.

(iv) The government may borrow funds in order to feed the enterprise deficits. As the public debt rises, the costs of servicing it increase and the overall budget position may worsen, calling for one of the earlier-mentioned measures. The interest payments go to enrich, on the whole, the relatively better-off sections of the community. The distributional merit of this consequence has, therefore, to be weighed against any similar merits of the enterprise policies leading to deficits.

(v) We have so far assumed a budget deficit at the government level. What happens if the condition is one of a budget surplus? As the deficit is met, the budget surplus declines, setting in motion curtailments in the repayments of public debt, restricting the chances of tax-reducing strategies, and affecting the prospect of certain public (and social) expenditures being undertaken by the government. To the extent that these effects stand in the way of distributional benefits being realized by the relatively poor sections of people, the net effects are to be considered as unsatisfactory. Whether these are an acceptable trade-off, nevertheless, for the initial round of benefits enjoyed by certain sections from the enterprise policies, is a question for evaluation in this case.

A few concluding observations may now be made. Public enterprise deficits, of which some may be the result of distributional policies, eventually lead to a discrimination against taxpayers as a whole and to discriminations among taxpayer groups. The relative merits of the enterprise policies need to be determined in the knowledge of the final effects at the taxation end.

Where the distributional value of the enterprise policies is itself in doubt, as in the case of indiscriminate price softness, the odds in eventual evaluation, taking the tax effects also into account, are most likely to be against the propriety of those policies.

The discussion suggests that the qualifications to the merits of enterprise policies promotive of distributional justice are so heavy that one should be highly circumspect in permitting such policies. At least two reasons may be mentioned. First, the pursuit of such policies having the effect of deficits can be abused by an enterprise as a shield for a wide range of managerial inefficiencies. Second, there can be a positive advantage in the government insisting that the enterprise make a surplus and turn it over to the government, so that the government, in its right, decides on its utilization in the interest of distributional equity. This is the central point of the next section.

Direct budget expenditures

This section does not intend to cover such questions as whether the government should undertake distributional measures and within what limits such measures should be devised. It is limited to a review of the comparative merits of direct government expenditures as an alternative to public enterprise policies aimed at distributional equity.

(a) There is, first, the simple case of a public enterprise not pursuing distributional policies in any deliberate manner; either because it is unwilling to do so or because it cannot satisfactorily do so. Now there is no choice for the government except to initiate distributional measures through its own budget strategy, assuming that it is determined to promote a given pattern of income redistributions.

(b) Let us turn to cases where a public enterprise can implement, on its own volition, or can be made to implement distributional policies through input and pricing policies. In what respects will the alternative of direct measures by the government in the implementation of distributional policies be commendable?

(i) In many cases public enterprise policies tend to operate in an indiscriminate manner, in the sense that leakages of benefit occur in favour of the less deserving. Plugging this through sophisticated devices of linking the policies exclusively to the deserving classes of people, as intended, may prove too difficult in practice. Besides, the rationale as well as the element of enforceability of such devices has to be derived ultimately from the government. It may be preferable for the government itself directly to undertake measures that are capable of offering the selfsame distributional benefits to the identified classes of people.

(ii) Direct distributional measures by the government have another substantive merit. A policy pursued by, say, a gas enterprise has benefits, by and large, exclusively for its clientele — mainly its own workers and its own consumers. It does not benefit similarly poor consumers of other forms of energy, for example, coal or electricity. It is possible, besides, that these other enterprises implement policies, perhaps unwittingly, that are in fact antisocial in effect: for instance, an electricity enterprise may announce prices that decline as the size of consumption increases, favouring large and rich consumers. From the national point of view, assuming that distributional measures in the *energy* area are decided upon, the real aim should be to assist the low-income brackets in the context of energy consumption, rather than in terms of individual substitute products. This can only be achieved by appropriate measures at the government level. (The crudest consists of the grant of a cash subsidy from the public exchequer to the identified poor at so much per unit of energy consumption within a ceiling).

We can formulate different versions of the relative merit enunciated in the preceding paragraph. The distributional policies of an enterprise may operate in favour of its workers rather than its consumers. (Enough empirical suspicion exists in this respect.) The reasons for the policy on the part of the enterprise may range over the following: buying industrial peace, workers' demands for reward under conditions of monopoly, managerial logistics that incorporate worker influence in decision making, and weakness of consumer organizations. If such a result is considered antisocial on macro grounds, one vehicle for remedying it would be direct governmental interventions in parcelling out distributional benefits.

Yet another version comes from an extension of this picture. Where the groups that enjoy the distributional benefits of the policies of an enterprise (workers and consumers put together) do not represent the least well-to-do sections of the population, the result is questionable from the national angle of distributional equity. This can be remedied if the government directly assumes the role of offering distributional benefits in a selective way on macro grounds.

Further, many governments have begun to adopt the 'basic needs' approach in the context of their strategies of planned development. For instance, the Kenya Development Plan for 1984–8 states that 'basic needs, such as education, food, security, nutrition, water, health care, housing, and law and order, require a fair allocation of national resources, both public and private'.[3] The Indian Plan for 1980–5 refers to the 50 per cent of the population 'living below the poverty line'.[4] Many of the remedial measures are such as can most appropriately be taken by the government directly, as evidenced by the emphasis placed by the Plan on the Intregrated Rural Development Programme, the National Rural Employment Programme, and the Special Component Plan for the uplift of scheduled castes. This does not negate the justifiability of select entrustment of implementation to either existing public enterprises[5] or to new creations intended to discharge, with operational expertise, specified governmental functions.[6] (A few non-enterprises in an autonomous organizational form do exist in many countries already.[7]) This point will be picked up again in chapter 5.

(iii) There is an institutional or administrative reason in support of direct government expenditures. It may be recalled that at several points in the earlier chapters we recognized the propriety of guidelines on the distributional policies being derived from, and meaningfully communicated by, the government to the enterprise managers. We know from global experience that this is seldom achieved satisfactorily. The alternative of direct government implementation eliminates this problem. Decisions emerge through due process of parliamentary discussion or in some other way in the normal routine of government procedures. And the contingency of enterprise managers assuming the role of wilful distributional arbiters is minimized.

(c) A brief comment may be made on the problem of resources for the government in the context of direct distributional expenditures. It is possible that the funds otherwise transferable to public enterprises making deficits through distributional policies are available for direct utilization by the government in implementing budget policies formulated on macro considerations. Further it would be desirable to work out formulae for the transfer of a part of public enterprise profits to the exchequer — on grounds which go beyond the point of discussion; and the government's resources for direct distributional expenditures will be improved as a result.

Chapter five

The Aggregate Effects

So far our discussion has proceeded in terms of the policies of individual public enterprises. There are certain distributional effects that flow from the very institution of public enterprise; and their significance varies with the size of the public enterprise sector. They are also influenced by its composition.

The size of the public enterprise sector

Let us look, first, at the aggregate size of the public enterprise sector in the national economy in relative terms. The theme is that in an economy that has a relatively large size of public enterprise the scope for certain 'intrinsic' effects with a distributional bias is great, as evidenced by the objectives mentioned in support of the large-scale nationalizations undertaken in Pakistan consequent on the promulgation of the Economic Reforms Order.[1]

The effects have their genesis in the fact that public enterprise implies that investment ownership is not in private hands. The rewards of investment reach the government where the enterprises are owned by it fully. In this way the opportunities for private investors to lay their hands on the surpluses are more restricted, the more considerably the larger the aggregate size of public enterprise in the national economy. A good result ensues, from the distribution angle, if it is assumed that the private profits go to enrich the relatively wealthy sections of the population on the whole — probably true in many economies where great skewness exists in shareholding and wealth distribution. Moreover public enterprises would have the opportunity, if permitted, of utilizing their surpluses for the benefit of the low-income brackets among their clientele.

It is true that a large part of public enterprise investments has been derived from public borrowings in the first place — certainly at the initial stages. The private lenders receive interest incomes. But these are likely to be lower, though steadier, than the profits that the investments produce. Thus there is a margin of gain for the public sector. This margin rests with the enterprises, assuming that they received capital from the government at the (low) rates that correspond to those on public borrowings;

and this can be used for whatever distributional policies the enterprises may (or may be induced to) implement.

If, on the other hand, the government borrows funds at a low rate but then lends them to public enterprises at rates near enough to the market rates, the enterprises will be left with rather narrow margins of profit after interest; the margins are substantially left with the government which can decide on their budgetary use. The opportunity that profits offer the enterprises to pursue distributional policies will be limited, as compared with the earlier circumstance.

If public enterprises go directly to capital markets and commit themselves to the market rates of interest, their 'profit–minus–interest' margins will be lower than in the earlier cases; and so will be their opportunities for pursuing distributional policies.

The strength of the argument depends on the assumption that public enterprises raise substantial profits, so that after the interest payments are made, sizable margins remain with them. Unfortunately, this assumption is of doubtful validity, as per several empirical studies including a recent IMF compilation of net finances data in the public enterprise sector for many countries.[2]

If public enterprises, in the aggregate, present a deficit such that even the cost of capital used can only be met from the public exchequer, there will be an outflow of benefits from the taxpayer to the lenders. The larger the public enterprise sector and the larger the aggregate deficit, the greater this flow, which involves a distributional sequence in reverse of what was presented in the foregoing argument.

Reverting to the prospect of a surplus situation in the public enterprise sector, we can deduce an additional good result from the distribution angle. As surpluses are made over years, the capital worth of the enterprises increases. That is, appreciations in the value of ownership occur. And these will vest in the government as owner. In this way a major channel of private enrichment in the corporate sector is plugged. The benefit goes to the taxpayer, or to workers and consumers of public enterprises under certain conditions.

The next chapter will cover certain other allied aspects of the problem under discussion.

The composition of the public enterprise sector

The sectoral composition of public enterprise is of relevance in a review of its distributional implications.

Where the majority of the investments in public enterprise go into infrastructural and basic industries, they have a unique purport for the distributional outcomes. In the first place, their overriding motivation is one of growth; emphasis on distributional results may take a secondary place. The operational policies of the enterprises may tend to be neutral to the idea of conferring benefits on chosen groups of the low-income brackets. Brazil is a typical case in point, where the public enterprises in basic industry and public utilities have not pursued the social objective of employment creation.[3] The focus has been on a fast pace of industrial growth.[4]

Most of the investments are likely to be in upstream activities; and the outputs are sold to intermediate consumers. Thus the opportunities of implementing direct benefits to poor consumers are restricted. Any possible distributional outcomes are traceable to the secondary rounds of product distribution, as discussed in chapter 3 (see pp 56-58).

The cross section of basic and heavy categories of public enterprises have not been surplus oriented. Irrespective of the correctness of policy, governments have tended to bring them within low profit yielding lines of input and output strategy. Most activities belonging to the sector of consumer goods have, by and large, remained outside the core of the public enterprise sector in many mixed economies. This has deprived it of the opportunity of accumulating a surplus without such constraints as surround the basic and infrastructural sectors.

One other characteristic of public enterprise in most mixed economies has been high capital intensity — partly because it has predominantly covered high-technology activities. This can have a double — possibly not positive — distributional effect. The scope for employing a 'large' labour force is limited, unless deliberate overmanning is pursued (as evidenced in some countries in practice); and rewards to the suppliers of capital tend to attract a relatively high proportion of the factor incomes.

An important limitation on the distributional potentialities of public enterprise so far could be traced to its non-coverage of activities most pertinent to the offering of reliefs to the low-income brackets or to the most poverty-ridden sections of the community. As mentioned elsewhere in this study, activities in rural areas in such local-oriented sectors as agriculture, fishing, cottage industry, sanitation, and other public works do not yet constitute a prominent part of the public enterprise sector; and it is in agriculture that in most countries relatively large numbers are engaged with relatively low wage incomes.[5] (In Botswana, for example, 89.3 per cent of the population is rural;[6] 'the average urban household's income is more than twice that of the average rural household'.[7]

This problem is being realized gradually; and governments are attaching effective meaning to the 'basic needs' approach in relieving poverty. (Earlier citations from the Indian Plan illustrate the point.) What is likely, however, is that certain modifications will prove necessary to the idea of 100 per cent public ownership, in the interests of operational efficiency. Some contracting-out may be desirable, wherever private

Aggregate effects

contractees can fulfil a production or marketing function advantageously and economically. Also the co-operative principle of organization may be judiciously introduced into the public sector, attracting the actual producers — farmers, fishermen, workers, artisans, etc. — into the organizational system. (A good example is provided by the state of Andhra Pradesh in India, where the government investments cover public enterprises as well as co-operative enterprises, though the latter, as a percentage, is low.) In these ways there can be better modalities of positive distributional effects through guaranteed wage incomes for, as well as some profit-sharing by, the poorest sections of people. To put it in another way, as governments progressively turn towards such investments, the public investment sector, in effect, moves towards regions of poverty, touching a clientele sunk in poverty. Of course, as a proportion of total public enterprise investments, these are not likely to be high; but they can be less low than of now, with a better guarantee of positive distributional effects.

Appendix 5.1 Dualism in income distribution

The data drawn from Lecaillon et al. (1984)[8] refer to twelve developing countries of Africa, Latin America, and Asia:

1. Ivory Coast   (1970)
2. Madagascar   (1970)
3. Senegal   (1970)
4. Swaziland   (1974)
5. Zambia   (1972)
6. Colombia   (1972)
7. Mexico   (1968)
8. Iran   (1972)
9. Republic of Korea (1970)
10. Malaysia   (1967)
11. Philippines   (1961)
12. Turkey   (1970)

The years in parentheses denote the years to which the data refer. In figure 5.1 the x-axis represents the percentage of the agricultural sector out of the total economically active persons and the y-axis represents the percentage of the agricultural sector out of the total incomes. Each point in the graph represents, for *a* country, the relationship between relative employment and relative income in the agricultural sector. Very clearly all the points occur below the equiproportional diagonal, indicating dualism in income distribution unfavourable to the agricultural sector. In particular the countries with the highest proportions of occupants in agriculture stand the farthest below the equiproportional diagonal.

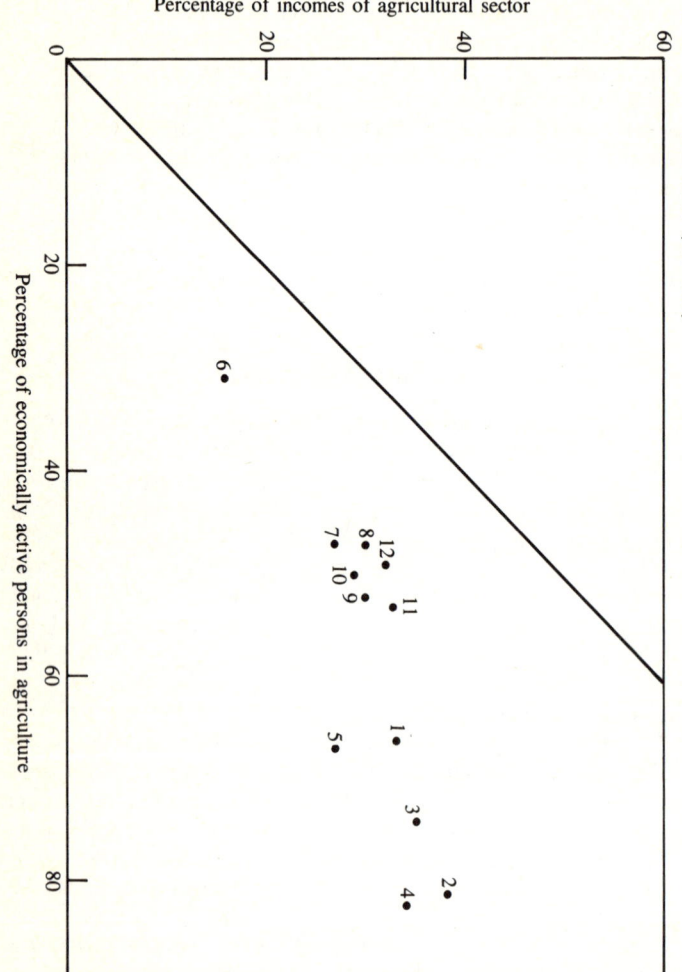

Figure 5.1 Employment and incomes in the agricultural sector in twelve countries (see text)

Chapter six

Privatization and Income Distribution

Introduction

The privatization of public enterprise has been among the policy options for economic well-being in developed countries and of development strategy in developing countries in recent years. Active implementation has been in progress in substantial measure in the UK and France; while serious thought is being given to the appropriateness of privatization and its modalities in countries in all regions, for example, Kenya, Peru, Sri Lanka, and Jamaica. This chapter seeks to analyze the distributional implications of privatization, with reference, first, to the sale transaction, second, to the cash inflow into the public exchequer, and finally, to the long-term perspective.

At the outset reference may be made to a distribution-oriented argument in favour of privatization, namely, that the record of public enterprise as a cross section in promoting the socially preferred results of income and/or wealth distribution has not been satisfactory, and that, in several cases, the results have been positively anti-distributional through the disproportionate accrual of benefits to the upper-income brackets. Hence, it is argued, privatization can put an end to the shifts of benefit or income considered inequitable in the context of a given situation; for the privatized enterprises would not be interested in other than commercial operations, and would, unlike public enterprise managers, be free from governmental pressures to adopt deliberate input, output, and investment policies aimed at certain distributional goals, as against the goal of profit.

Two qualifications suggest themselves. First, there is no reason why a reasonably effective attempt cannot be made to keep a public enterprise from the pursuit of distributional policies, except under a transparent arrangement with the government. Second, it cannot be asserted that, when privatized, the operations of the enterprise will be completely innocent of distributional consequences of one kind or another.

A prefatory note on the concept of privatization[1] would be helpful. It represents a continuum of measures, at one end of which lies denationalization in ownership terms. It is to this (i.e. denationalization) that the present discussion refers. Extensive data from the UK experience are used in this chapter with the purpose of illustrating a point or building up an argument and not for providing a critique of that experience *per se*.

The sale implications

The level of sale price fixed or realized for the assets which are privatized determines whether the taxpayer has had a rough deal, to the advantage of the buyer. If the sale proceeds tend to be 'low', the private investors enjoy a benefit; and if, on an average, they belong to richer income brackets than the average taxpayer, the transaction contains distributionally unsatisfactory elements. The sale prices tend to be low when: (a) the government is anxious to sell the assets (or enterprise) and vindicate that privatization can be (and is) effected successfully; (b) the modality of sale implies lower fixed prices than tenders would produce, and higher commissions to underwriters and 'city merchants' than are necessary; (c) the enterprise is not sufficiently prepared or restructured to attract relatively high bids from buyers; and/or (d) the government proclaims some preference for the 'small' subscriber in whose interest the sale price is set lower than is otherwise possible.

The UK experience since 1980 amply evidences all these phenomena that culminated in the inflow into the public exchequer of sale proceeds that fell far short of what could be reasonably expected. The considerable oversubscriptions in several cases (e.g. 'nine times the shares available' in the case of British Telecom[2]) illustrate the proposition, as also the far higher prices that instantly prevailed in the share market. (For example, 'on the first day of trading . . . dealing closed at 93p representing a premium of 43p on the partly paid shares . . . . The partly paid price subsequently varied between 87½p . . . and 166p'; and when 'trading switched on to a second instalment paid basis, trading . . . closed at 197p'. All this happened between 3 December 1984 and 28 May 1985.[3])

As may be gathered from the reports of Parliamentary Committees and the National Audit Office, the Government's 'main policy was to achieve a successful flotation';[4] 'the prime objective was the successful sale to the private sector of 49 per cent of the company's shares; maximization of the proceeds of sale, while extremely important, was a secondary consideration,'[5] 'That the extent of risk justified the rates agreed for placing commission' is not convincing, in the context of the British Telecom shares.[6] There was 'high cost of underwriting' in the case of Britoil shares.[7] The Department of Transport concluded that 'underwriting would be necessary because of the need to ensure the immediate sale of the full 49 per cent of the shares of Associated British Posts Holding plc'.[8] 'The expenditure on the controversial "Tell Sid" advertising campaign was needlessly high' in the case of British Gas.[9] Sealink may have been sold at a low price at a time when the value of the assets was 'depressed'.[10]

The data in table 6.1 illustrate the market premiums on shares, which represent the extent of transfers of benefit from the mute taxpayer to the smart share-allottee.

Table 6.1 Market premiums on shares

Enterprise (1)	Premium as on first-day close (2)	Premium as on 9 September 1987 (3)
British Telecom	+ 86%	+ 108%
Trustees Savings Bank	+ 71%	+ 164%
British Gas	+ 25%	+ 82%
British Airways	+ 68%	+ 58%
Rolls Royce	+ 73%	+ 32%
British Airports Authority	+ 46%	+ 33%

Financial Times Survey 16 September 1987, p. 11.

The amounts involved were very large. The loss to the exchequer or the taxpayer, through share underpricing, was over £300 million in the case of British Airways, to take one example, on an issue worth £900 million. This, no doubt, drew a subtle comment from the National Audit Office.

The comment is fairly common in the UK, that several privatizations have implied 'windfall gains for the investor at public expense';[11] that 'the taxpayer could have benefited further from the sale' of British Telecom shares;[12] and 'a loss to the economy as a whole' was caused in the case of British Aerospace, where the accumulated dividend obligation of £55 million was waived on the eve of its privatization so as not to affect its 'attractiveness to the market'.[13] On the seven sell-offs reviewed by the Trades Union Congress it estimated a £1.4 billion loss to taxpayers and mentioned reasons why it considered this to be an underestimate.[14]

France provides fewer instances of underpricing, except for such early cases as St Gobain; but its privatizations have so far referred mainly to competitive banking, and insurance sectors. We do not have well documented evidence on the privatizations elsewhere. However, as the argument goes, in developing countries, it would be difficult to adjudicate conclusively on the privatizations of losing or problematic enterprises; besides we cannot rule out subtle elements of underpricing traceable to certain non-transparent features of price-fixing or bargaining.

Let us turn to the features of wide ownership of privatized shares and share allotments to the 'small' applicants, widely publicized in several countries (e.g. the UK and Pakistan).[15] Apparently these produce distributionally good results, including the accrual to 'small' holders of any benefits of share underpricing at the expense of the exchequer and the taxpayer. On close analysis, several qualifications suggest themselves.

(i) Many of the allottees tend to sell away their shares 'at an immediate substantial premium' to secure 'windfall gains'.[16] Thus their continuing benefits from future profits are capitalized. Whether their sale receipts go into investment elsewhere is doubtful. In several cases the moneys are used to liquidate the credits (from banks) which they took for buying the shares. Their involvement in the privatized enterprise is limited to raising a capital gain through quick exit from the shareholders' register.

This has characterized several privatizations in the UK. For example, within the space of a year after flotation 'individual shareholders fell by 83 per cent; and the decline in the number of 'small' shareholders with less than 100 shares each was by 93 per cent.[17] The stage for ownership concentration, the familiar feature of private corporate business, was already set.

(ii) If 'small' ownership is significant in terms of capital, rather than numbers, one can hope that the good distributional result of ownership deconcentration will be realized. Experience suggests that it is not so. The skewness in ownership can be illustrated with reference to the shareholding sizes in the privatized industries.[18] One can argue that it is not wealthy individuals only that hold large blocks of shares; financial institutions, pension funds, etc. are important holders, no doubt. The distributional effects of such a shareholding structure would then be a function of how the eventual benefits of the operations of those institutions happen to be. To the extent that they reach the higher-income brackets through whatever channel, the element of skewness in the enjoyment of equity-holding benefits continues to exist.

Skewness in shareholding seems to be a common feature of many countries. For example, 80 per cent of stocks belong to only 200 families in Pakistan; Chile's privatization programme has brought back ownership concentration;[19] and it is feared that 'the half-dozen leading private sector groups' might be the only buyers of privatized units in Italy.[20]

(iii) Is the 'small' allottee relatively small 'income-wise'? Though a conclusive answer is difficult, there are two points worth noting. First, one who is allotted a small number of shares in a privatized enterprise may also be a holder of shares in other enterprises, including other privatized enterprises. The allottee is not necessarily 'small' as a holder of share capital. Second, in many developing countries, the 'small' allottee does not belong to the poorest income brackets which consist, predominantly, of the rural population, agricultural labour, workers in the informal sector, and large numbers of the unemployed.

(iv) A special case of the smallness argument is that the employees of the privatized enterprises have been offered shares under relatively soft terms, as illustrated by the British Aerospace case[21] and more recently by the British Airports Authority (BAA).[22] Apparently fair, this practice raises the issue that public enterprise employees are not among the lowest-income brackets, especially in developing countries, as mentioned earlier.

In any case employee shareholding is most unlikely to constitute a device of ownership deconcentration, especially in non-labour-intensive and large-sized enterprises. The UK data confirm this proposition. Roughly the proportions of total issued capital initially held by employees were as follows:[23]

British Aerospace	3.6%
Cable and Wireless	1.4%
Amersham International	3.7%
Britoil	0.1%
Associated British Ports	4.3%
Enterprise Oil	0.03%
Jaguar	1.3%
British Telecom	1.99%

One may argue that preferential share offers to employees are not uncommon in the private sector. But there is an asymmetry. There the decision is taken, and the consequences of cheap offer borne, by the private owners. On the other hand, the underrealization of sale proceeds that this involves are borne, in the case of a public enterprise, by the taxpayer and prompt the question of distributional equity implicit in such a consequence.

In conclusion, the efficacy of privatization in the distributional context is doubtful, (a) if it provides windfall gains to the share-allottees who dispose of their shares at a high profit, (b) if it assures continuing benefits of high returns on initial investment to those that have not resold their shares, and (c) if the major part of the share capital is owned by large shareholders. On the whole, if benefits of ownership were to be made available to the largest numbers, public ownership would be a better means than privatization. But there could be forceful arguments, other than those based on distributional grounds, against public ownership, case by case.

The exchequer implications

The next major issue under privatization which has distributional relevance, is the way in which the cash that comes into the exchequer is utilized. In theory, it is available for any of the following purposes or in any combination of them:

(i) *To meet budget deficits.* Tax increases may be set aside, expenditure cuts relaxed, additions to public debt reduced, and deficit-financing curbed. If it is assumed that the taxes not increased are the relatively regressive taxes, that the expenditures not cut are the relatively social or welfare expenditures, and that additional borrowings might be accompanied by additional regressive taxes, the results of the cash inflow would be compatible with distributional criteria.

(ii) *To offer tax cuts.* Here much depends on whom the tax cuts benefit. While in the developed countries like the UK the benefit may be widely spread, in most developing countries income-taxpayers are a small proportion of the population. The benefit of tax cuts might be broad-based only if they related to indirect taxes affecting the consumption basket of the generality of population, accompanied by the necessary controls against producers and middle-men mopping up the margins.

(iii) *To undertake increased current expenditures.* Once again the distributional implications depend on the nature of the expenditures and their geographical distribution. If more is spent than otherwise might be on public services such as education, health, rural electrification, and provision of drinking water, either by extending the size of the services or by improving the elements of free or cheap supply, *and* if a major proportion of the expenditures goes towards items of direct benefit to the low-income brackets and in regions of relative poverty, the results can be considered to be satisfactory from the distributional angle. But if the increases occur elsewhere, few of the benefits would accrue to the less well-to-do sections of the population.

There is a common feature of the three measures mentioned above, namely, that they imply the utilization of a capital inflow into the public exchequer, for purposes of current expenditure. There will come a time when the current benefits received by given groups of people will dry up, other things being equal, as the one-time receipts supporting them are exhausted. Besides, the benefits that taxpayers across the board were receiving from the annual inflow of public enterprise surpluses into the exchequer before privatization would not be there, since their source itself is disposed of and dissipated for current purposes. And the budget impacts on the low-income brackets are likely to reappear. (Further sales of government assets may only defer the consequence somewhat.)

(iv) *To reduce the public debt.* Either through debt repayments or through reduced fresh borrowings, this has the merit of applying a capital inflow to a capital purpose, as the French Government has significantly been doing.[24] The effects that flow from this practice, at least the first round, may be traced as follows.

To the extent that funds are used by the government to reduce public debt, the resources available in private hands — in the aggregate — for earning a return remain the same as before privatization; for, whatever cash they paid for buying shares comes back. But there is a difference. These resources were earning an interest, fixed and relatively low, whereas they will have the opportunity of earning flexible rates of profit. Assuming that their investment choice in acquiring shares in a privatized enterprise is right and that the enterprise retains a fair degree of monopoly power, they will end up with a difference of income in their favour, taking one year with another. And the skewness in the distribution of profit incomes in the economy gets intensified.

In so far as the exchequer is concerned, there will be a recurring loss of income equal to the excess of the dividend/profit income that an erstwhile public enterprise was bringing over the interest outgoings attributable to the related figure of public debt. The distributional effects of this loss are to be analysed in terms of the budget policies adopted to deal with it, as discussed earlier. Briefly, if cuts in social expenditures and/or increases in regressive taxes occur, the relatively poor will be adversely affected.

It is likely that the loss of income that the exchequer sustains through profits foregone will be moderated to the extent that the additions to private gains attract income or corporate taxation. (There may be heavy tax evasions in certain countries, though.)

It may be noted that the underlying assumption in the preceding paragraphs is that the enterprise in question was bringing into the exchequer profit incomes in excess of the interest implications of the related public debt. If it was not, and yet it *was* earning profits that exceeded the bare interest charges, the net surpluses must have been either reinvested or used for wage or price benefits. In the former case the nature of distributional effects that follow, though not directly from the budget, depends on the character of the reinvestments pursued by the public enterprise. And in the latter case the outcomes relevant to income distribution depend on what income brackets the wage enhancements or price reductions benefit.

Where the erstwhile public enterprise was not contributing profits to the exchequer and was not raising surpluses at all, the situation seems to be somewhat complicated. If the exchequer was receiving at least enough to meet its interest commitments on the related amount of public debt, the only fresh distributional effects would be those attributable to the profit incomes of the shareholders of the privatized enterprise in excess of their earlier interest incomes. If the exchequer was not receiving from the enterprise the due interest incomes in full, or if it had to offer subsidies to meet its deficits, one may consider the privatization as a gentle riddance from the exchequer angle. But it does have a disguised effect on the budget. The sale price of the enterprise would be low enough to reflect the profit-and-loss position of the enterprise, so much so that the exchequer sustains a capital loss on the sale. That is, the sale proceeds that flow in would be less than the related figure of public debt; and servicing the debt balance will be a recurring problem, with its own tax and expenditure consequences. (Perhaps this might be cheaper for the exchequer in the long run.)

This is the situation most frequently encountered in many developing countries. Appropriate financial restructuring is generally postponed, almost *sine die*, thereby inflating the enterprise losses and public subsidies of an open or disguised nature. All the time the distributional inequities that eventually flow from the inherent problems get aggravated. In breaking such a vicious circle privatization could be a commendable option which undoubtedly reflects the erosion of public capital that *has* occurred.

(v) *To undertake capital expenditures*. These can fall into three categories: those that are social-welfare-oriented; those that constitute revenue-raising investments (as planned, in part, in France in 1986–7[25]) and others. A point common to all these categories is that the budget burdens of servicing the public debt attributable to the enterprise or assets privatized stay, unrequited by cash inflows in the shape of interest or profit (dividend). Certain distributional consequences follow from that situation. It may change favourably if the capital expenditures are intended to add to social welfare, for example, hospitals, schools, or housing which benefit the low-income brackets in particular.

Where the capital expenditures take the shape of surplus-raising investments, their financial results, by hypothesis, will neutralize the initial current income losses to the budget; and the distributional effects of the new profits will be similar to those traceable to the pre-privatization profit incomes of the exchequer. A further point of relevance is whether the operations of the enterprise(s) into which the new investments go will be capable of producing more favourable income effects for the workers, consumers, and low-income brackets in general than the former investments did. This is a matter of particular significance in the case of developing countries. For, a large segment of their public enterprises which offer themselves as fit candidates for privatization probably have few distributional merits; and the governments may decide to invest the sale proceeds in directions that are capable of benefiting the 'small' man: for example, small industry financing, irrigation projects, house-loan societies, and building contract organizations.

It will be realistic to recognize that, even within the limited extent of denationalization that many a developing country pursues, the direction of budgetary use of the sale proceeds is likely to tilt towards some kind of fresh investments. For, the need for public investments in certain sectors will still be there, on grounds that include the promotion of distributional equity. In other words, privatization can be a means of investment rotation in the public sector.

The third category of capital expenditures, illustrated by defence, space research, and new capital cities, is likely to be neutral to the distributional theme, by and large, except for its employment effects, which may be too limited in most cases.

We may conclude this section with a few comments on the effects of privatization sales on the size and pattern of investments in the economy and on their distributional implications.

If the total amount paid by the buyers of privatized assets comes back through public debt redemptions, there will be no effect on the size and perhaps the pattern of investments in the economy; hence no fresh implications from the distributional angle. If the funds that come back to the private sector through public debt redemptions are lower than the amounts transferred to the exchequer, but if the government invests the difference, the size of aggregate investment remains constant, but the pattern changes to the extent that the government's investments vary in criteria from those of private investments. As argued earlier, the government segment of investments can have distributional implications in some cases, favourable or otherwise.

If the government uses the sale proceeds partly for public debt redemption and partly for current purposes, the aggregate size of investment in the economy is likely to be affected unfavourably, except for two counteracting circumstances. First, the 'current purposes' may be such as provide a stimulus to investment (e.g. tax reductions); and second, the privatization schemes may contain elements that persuade some conversion of consumption into investment — not temporarily for quick gains, but on a long-term basis. The net effect on the size, rather than the pattern, depends on the interaction of those circumstances; so do the benefits of employment, wage incomes, and profit accruals.

If privatizations have the spill-out of 'small' men developing the investment habit, and if this effect stays, there can be some hope that small-sized dividend incomes will become more important than before. These can be considered as representing a favourable development from the distributional angle.

It may be noted that in the above discussion the possibility of a certain part of the privatization proceeds being derived from foreign investors has been kept out. If it is assumed that the foreign money which comes in for buying privatized assets would not have otherwise been invested in the economy, it eases the 'crowding-out' implications correspondingly, and the effects of privatization on the size of aggregate investment would be less restrictive than those indicated above. It would be realistic to assume that some foreign investment would have been there, irrespective of the privatization measures, though it would be difficult to estimate it precisely. It is only the 'extra' that is relevant to our argument.

When foreign capital acquires significant proportions of capital of privatized enterprises, as in several cases in West African countries, there is a unique potential for distributional concern. Both the managerial behaviour towards profit maximization and the repatriations of profits and certain other incomes, even if by subtle devices, could have unfavourable consequences for the workers, the consumers, and the economy in general. It is doubtful if corrective controls will be introduced by the government which, in the first place, invites foreign capital for achieving successful privatization.

Long-term implications

In a sense a privatized enterprise has the same implications for income distribution in the long run as private enterprise, in general, has. However, in this section a brief look is taken at any differences that may exist.

Any price structures which the enterprise adopted prior to privatization in the interest of income distribution would disappear gradually, if they vitiated against profit criteria. In the same way price differentials among markets which turned out to be anti-distributional in effect whatever their initial motivation, would also disappear if they ran counter to profit criteria. However, it is likely that public pressures prevail in favour of preserving certain price and output policies assumed to be in the interest of the poor consumer or in the national interest in some way; and at least for satisfying such a public attitude the regulatory structures may incorporate conditions that, in effect, permit the continuance of certain former non-profit-oriented practices. These, in ultimate analysis, fall into two categories.

(i) If the concessional prices entail losses (or if any outputs are made available free) the enterprise is expected to contain them through what amount to cross-subsidizations within its price structure. For example, it is visualized that the proposed Water Service Public Limited Companies (WSPLs) to be transferred to private ownership in the UK will continue to undertake some 'desirable activities . . .' at a loss; 'and that they will be able to meet the net cost of these services from the main service charges'.[26]

(ii) Where internal cross-subsidizations are not accorded approval by the Monopolies and Mergers Commission or any other control agencies acting at the instance of the affected consumers, arrangements have to be made for an open subsidy from the Government. An appropriate subsidy will be agreed as between the enterprise and the Government in such cases, and the anticipated good results from the distributional angle will emerge from public support.[27] And this would be a subject of legislative decision at the appropriate level.

The income benefits that the employees may have derived in the pre-privatization days through surplus employment, relatively high wages, incentive payments, and welfare perquisites, would gradually be levelled to what happen to be common to private enterprises in a given sector, assuming that labour markets are sufficiently perfect. To the extent that the privatized enterprise enjoys monopoly power the employees are likely to exercise their bargaining power in improving their incomes; and there might be some shift of benefits from the consumers if prices went up as a result. If governmental controls prevent price enhancements, the benefits that the workers amass may be derived from the recipients of profits.

In general, it would be easier for a privatized enterprise to close an uneconomical plant or introduce an economical change in its production function involving cuts in the labour force, than it was for the enterprise while in the public sector. As a consequence the wage-employment benefits that labour had enjoyed would diminish — rightly, if they were not derived from a transparent subsidy from the government — subject to the strength of its bargaining power in a given situation of product markets.

One concluding observation. Most of the natural monopolies would retain a significant degree of monopoly power even after privatization; as would enterprises in sectors where entry is highly imperfect. The list would be large in developing countries where markets are small and constraints on entrepreneurship are considerable. In theory the owners of the enterprises can be prevented from enjoying high profits. It is not clear how efficacious controls would be in practice and whether price controls of the 'RPI minus X' variety adopted in the UK would be adequate. The situation must have been the same when the enterprise had been in the public sector, except for a silver lining in the cloud: the profits that filtered through weak controls went, eventually, to the benefit of the exchequer, that is, the taxpayer, even if through the channel of self-financing. Thus, one may suggest that where privatization simply substitutes a private monopoly for a public monopoly, the distributional results can be unsatisfactory in that the profit earners may be a more probable beneficiary of the change than the wage earners or the consumers, on balance.

Chapter seven

Conclusion

A résumé

This study has sought to establish the nature of distributional implications of public enterprise operations. These have been examined primarily in terms of the policies of individual enterprises. The three major channels — wages (and input policies in general), pricing, and financial surplus/deficit — have been discussed at length, bringing out the deliberate as well as unintended or incidental results of enterprise policies. A special facet of the discussion has been to analyze who gains a distributional benefit and who yields it. The problems encountered in identifying the answers to these questions have been mentioned, as have the crucial aspects of (unintended) leakages of distributional benefits under each channel.

The study has been rounded off with a discussion on the relevance of the aggregate size and composition of the public enterprise sector in the national economy, in the context of income and wealth distribution; and with an analysis of the distributional implications of privatization, a popular current policy in many countries.

The thrust of the study has been analytical. Empirical references were introduced for illustration or for building up an argument in a real-world background.

The analysis, along with the indicative purport of the illustrative material, however, prompts us to speculate a few broad conclusions.

Of all the channels open to public enterprises, 'wages' could be and have been the most impactful in offering distributional benefits,[1] though it is questionable whether the wage beneficiaries of public enterprises, on the whole, are among the lowest-income brackets in the country.

The 'pricing' channel would be and has been of limited effect, what with its indiscriminateness and distributional leakages. Its applicability in the interest of an identified poor end consumer has yet been minimal in most public enterprise sectors. There are inherent difficulties in using pricing as a distributional tool.

The nearly universal fact of poor financial returns of public enterprises supports the possibility of fairly unfavourable implications in the distributional context (whatever good results of 'growth' may have been achieved in the process).

Turning to the aggregate effects of public enterprise as an institution, we have seen that, in theory, these could be positive, but we have also noted the reasons why in practice these may have only minimally been realized.

As an undercurrent in the discussion the point was made that, other things being equal, the government (or the public exchequer) would be a better medium for distributional policies than public enterprises.

The government and distributional policies

The proposition attaching superiority to the government as a medium of distributional policies calls for an annotation. We come across such questions as the following: Does the government know what is distributionally desirable? Is the government likely to be efficient in implementing distributional measures? Does not 'government' imply, in practice, a time-specific collusion of political interests and pressure groups?

At one level of argument the answers to these questions can be unfavourable to the government on the broad basis that the 'government' is not superior to the 'market' in ordering income flows and that a 'deliberate' measure is not superior to the free flow of market forces.

But we face a unique complex of conditions in the real world — at least in a major part of the world. The 'market' is imperfect. Distributional disparities are alarming and have not been adequately set right by market forces. Governments do consciously plan the structure and pace of socio-economic development; and distributional justice is an explicit objective of policy in most cases. And experience has shown that 'deliberate' measures of a wide-ranging nature are adopted through taxes, subsidies, public expenditures, minimum wage legislation, support prices, anti-firing laws, and unemployment reliefs.

It is with this backdrop that we have to discuss the issue. Assuming that distributional measures are necessary and in deliberate design, the government would be a better level than a public enterprise, from which the policies may flow, for the following reasons.

(i) Being in the nature of value judgements, the policies can be determined at the level of the government, implying that the legislative and administrative checks and balances inherent in the system of government apply to this area. Whereas, the enterprise managers, whose remit is essentially 'commercial', turn out to be poor arbiters in this delicate field. In fact, not to concede them the privilege of distributional decisions helps in keeping them to market principles in input and output policies, as far as possible.

(ii) Since distributional policies, for the best results, are to be devised in terms of a comprehensive strategy, and since most elements of the strategy — as is clear from the examples of measures cited above — emanate from the public exchequer, the government should, logically, be the agency that determines appropriate measures on a national or macro basis. Whereas the managers of a public enterprise can, at best, think of their own clientele, whose distributional deserts may not be the most compelling in the economy as a whole.

(iii) Conceding that the government is a time-specific political institution, we have two points to consider. First, we get the government we deserve; and do we not all the time let it undertake multifarious policy determinations and measures which affect our lives? Why should we single out the distributional area as an exception? Second, how can we be certain that the managers of every public enterprise have more dispassionate and less partisan interests than the government of the day? Their in-built bias for profit can itself be a conflicting consideration.

However, there are two qualifications to the proposition that the government is superior to a public enterprise in implementing distributional measures.

First, all public expenditures (and tax and subsidy policies) do not invariably benefit the low-income brackets, nor are the benefits confined to them only. The prospect of distributional benefits in their favour depends on two factors. The first is the sectoral composition of the expenditures. For example, agriculture, education, and health contain high elements of 'progressivity' on the whole. Even here 'the kind of expenditure' is of utmost relevance.[2] And sectors such as transport, mining, energy, industry, trade, and services, receiving benefits of public expenditures, lead to relatively low distributional benefits.[3] The other factor consists of the degree of selectivity to a benefit through public expenditures or subsidy policies. Many government measures have 'more or less missed their target', to quote Lecaillon *et al.*, 'and have been of benefit partly or mainly to medium-income and high-income households'.[4] Investment incentives (aimed at growth and the stimulation of entrepreneurship) and cheap credits for agriculture and housing are among the obvious examples of indiscriminate or neutral measures from the income distribution point of view.

To sum up: the efficacy of governmental measures as a distributional device depends on the selectivity of the sector (or sub-sector in fact) and of the precise beneficiary. This notwithstanding, the government would be a superior level, as compared with a public enterprise, to devise the right instruments of the selectivity. Even where a public enterprise operates distributional policies, the guidelines on the selectivity have, ideally, to be derived by it 'externally' — from the government.

The other qualification to the superiority of the government as a distributional agency is that there can be cases where it would make for economy and efficiency to use a public enterprise as an instrument in implementing certain distributional policies of the government.

This proposition applies most validly to activities analogous to government operations which are endowed with an autonomous form of organization for the sake of operational efficiency, free from bureaucratic constraints. There are many such organizations all over the world. The Food Corporation of India illustrates the phenomenon. It was set up 'basically . . . to impart an element of stability in the prices of food grains and also allow reasonable prices to the farmers and to create adequate buffer stocks for ensuring food security in the country'.[5] The National Cereals and Produce Board of Kenya is another example.[6]

To cite an example from another region, Latin America, the giant CONASUPO mercantile enterprise, intended as 'a vehicle' in supplying low-cost goods to low-income consumers, is really 'a part of the government's social welfare programme as much as it is an effort to improve the functioning of the marketing system'.[7]

Besides, benefits of scale and specialization justify the choice of public enterprises in certain cases for implementing the distributional policies that the government has in mind. Where a distributional measure happens to be a marginal addition to the operations of an enterprise already engaged in a given line of production and marketing — such as electricity or housing — it could be an advantage to the government as well as the consumer to entrust it to the enterprise.

An interesting illustration may be drawn from Botswana where government policy is not to subsidize the urban consumer of electricity but to let the rural consumer draw electricity at rates below full costs. The supply function is entrusted to the electricity enterprise; but the Government underwrites the rural investments of the electricity enterprise *as part of its* overall rural development strategy. The capital is offered on a 'grant basis' and rural consumers are not charged capital depreciation[8].

To sum up: it would be unwise for the government totally to disfavour the instrumentality of public enterprises in achieving desired distributional ends. But this calls for the right links and administrative relationships between the government and public enterprises, broadly reserving policy enunciation and monitoring to the government. This issue will be pursued in the next section.

The institutional aspects

The distributional instrumentality of public enterprise has an institutional dimension that needs attention. This may be examined under four heads: (a) where the government introduces distributional motivations into the operations of a public enterprise; (b) where a public enterprise implements distribution policies on its own volition; (c) where any distributional implications of the policies of a public enterprise, even if not overtly intended, need to be identified; and (d) where a periodic overall evaluation includes an appraisal of the distributional results of the policies and operations of the enterprise.

(i) There are three facets of institutional concern in the first case, that is, where the government seeks to inject a distributional bias into the operations of a public enterprise. First, the sanction for the decision has to be clearly established. At the minimum, this presupposes a consensus among the parent ministry, the treasury, and the planning ministry. For, the considerations that go into the value judgements concerned and their relative weights have to emerge from these three sources. (Perhaps parliament may come into the picture as well at some stage in the case of the more basic determinations, especially those that concern inter-regional equity.) Second the determined biases have to be properly communicated to the enterprise. That is, there must be clarity as to which agency in the government issues the binding instruction or guideline; the transmission must be transparent; and it must be as meaningful (i.e. clear) as possible to the managers of the enterprise who have to translate the biases into input and output policies. Third, a system must be evolved for the financing of the net-revenue consequences of the distributional biases. There are two broad modalities, as already noted at several points of the study; there can be cross-subsidizations within the enterprise; or there can be a compensation (in some way) from outside. What the government prefers, or in what combination the government wishes both the channels to operate, has to be made clear in advance of the consequences.

(ii) Where the distributional policies are practised by an enterprise on its own volition, there is a public need for asking the enterprise to make a statement on the policies and offer any further information helpful in establishing the implications of the policies. Once the statement is available, there must be a system within the government to evaluate the propriety of the measures and the effects, through a consensus, as in the previous case, among the parent ministry, the treasury, and the planning ministry. The conclusions have to be transmitted to the enterprise in an enforceable way, so that (a) the permissible policies are distinguished from the rest, (b) the net-revenue consequences of the permissible policies attract the appropriate channels of finance, and (c) the non-permissible policies get effectively dismantled.

(iii) It is probable that in practice an enterprise may be reluctant to come forward with a statement on the distributional policies it has wilfully adopted; or it may present a minimal statement. In the nature of the problem, the need exists for the government to establish if any significant distributional effects flowed from whatever input and output policies an enterprise has pursued. This would be the starting point of public concern and would call for an organized effort to probe three areas:

(1) *Prices*: Under what conditions and at which disaggregated levels can given prices be described as so low or so high as to contain a distributional bias?

(2) *Wages*: How can the wage incomes offered by an enterprise be appraised in relation to some standard, so as to establish if they contain unique elements attributable to distributional bias?

(3) *Other input policies*: Do these (e.g. materials procurement through ancillaries) appear to contain distributional implications, as compared with alternatives across the market open to the enterprise?

These constitute the substantive core of the problem. Our interest at this point of the discussion is to suggest the nature of institutional requirements that this entails. First, who is to research into these rather difficult areas? A non-governmental agency, such as a Public Enterprise Commission[9] or a Monopolies Commission,[10] would be ideal for this purpose. The findings should go to the parent ministry and the treasury which, in consultation with the planning ministry, convey enforceable directions to the enterprise on any remedial action. And as regards the permissible segments of the distributional biases, the government should deal with the further problem of net-revenue consequences, as already discussed.

(iv) Independently of the three preceding situations, there would be need to cover the distributional aspects of the operations of a public enterprise as part of an overall evaluation of it undertaken periodically, say, once in four or five years. The facets to be reviewed should go beyond the substance of the earlier three stages and be directed towards the following questions:

(1) What more can be done, on macro grounds, so as to invest the operations of the enterprise with any desired distributional biases?

(2) What aspects of the distributional policies pursued by the enterprise would it be desirable to shift to the public exchequer, and vice versa?

(3) Do the distributional implications of its operations constitute an acceptable trade-off for any adverse impacts, implicitly, on 'growth' in any sense of the term?

Such a review can be a part of an evaluation exercise. It can also be undertaken as a distribution-oriented review touching an entire sector of activity or a region or all public enterprises. Such a comprehensive or cross sectional coverage has its own merits, in that it brings into the exercise potential clienteles of a whole sector, region, or public enterprise in its aggregate size and composition.

Such enquiries, it is needless to say, should be of an expert nature, constituted independently of government bureaucracy. However, the doubtful prospect of an overall enquiry — in fact there has not been one such in any country so far — should not be used as an excuse for indefinitely postponing action at any of the three other stages discussed above.

As in the earlier cases, the findings of the reviews should be followed by the emergence of a consensus among the parent ministry, the treasury, and the planning ministry; the transmission of enforceable directives or guidelines to the enterprises concerned; and an agreed system of financing the net-revenue consequences of the distributional policies remitted to the enterprises and declared as pursuable.

In conclusion, we may refer to the situation of public enterprise in an economy where it nearly covers the whole of the corporate sector. (There are quite a few illustrations of this phenomenon: Ethiopia, Somalia, Sudan, Egypt, Syria, Madagascar, Yemen, and all the centrally planned economies of Europe.) The pricing policies of the enterprises — as also the wage policies — tend to be under open or disguised influence of the government, the more so when directoral and managerial centralization exists in favour of the top government agencies. There may also be arrangements for profit-sharing between the government and the enterprises which have unequal impacts on the clienteles of the different enterprises — the workers and the consumers in particular. Finally, there may be diverse external financial limits or capital expenditures ceilings applicable to different enterprises; these have consequences for the size of operations, employment, and consumer interest. In all these situations, unless there is open discussion at the parliamentary level, the actions of the executive wing of the government are not exposed to parliamentary accountability. Yet distributional effects may be flowing from its actions. It is, therefore, especially necessary that the institutional requirements commended in the preceding sections (iii) and (iv) should be observed effectively in this case. Two good results can ensue: first, the officials of the government will themselves realize what distributional implications their policies have in practice, whether these were intended or not; and second, the public will have a chance of demanding the accountability of the executive wing to the public in some way in the context of any proclaimed goals of distributional equity.

Notes

1. The nature of the problem

1. A United Nations study on 'Planning for Development' highlights that 'what distinguishes the current plans from their early predecessors in an important respect is the enhanced attention given to the need for alleviating imbalances between different population groups and between different geographical regions within countries'. (1977) *Journal of Development Planning* no. 11:23).
2. For instance, Fiji's *Seventh Development Plan 1976–80* (p.5) stresses the achieving of a more equitable distribution of the fruits of development. Also see Morocco *Plan de Developpement Economique et Sociale 1973–74*. The government intends that 'moroconization' of the national economy will not be for the sole benefit of the wealthiest but will be an instrument for favourable distribution of income.
3. Pakistan (1970) *The Fourth Five Year Plan 1970–5*, Islamabad, p.19.
4. Nigeria *Third National Development Plan 1975–80*, vol. I, Lagos, p.35.
5. Sri Lanka (1971) *The Five Year Plan 1972–6*, Colombo, p.2.
6. India, Planning Commission *Draft Fifth Five Year Plan 1974–9*, vol. I, New Delhi, p.22.
7. India, Planning Commission *Sixth Five Year Plan 1980–5*, New Delhi, p.34.
8. The Imperial Government of Iran (1965) *Outline of the Third Plan 1941–6*, Teheran, p.91.
9. The Imperial Government of Iran (1975) *A Summary of Iran's Fifth National Development Plan 1973–8. Revised*, Teheran, p.6.
10. ibid., p.7.
11. ibid., p.7.
12. Kuwait, the Planning Board (1968) *The First Five Year Development Plan 1967/8–1971/2*, Kuwait, p.8.
13. Government of Pakistan, Planning Commission *Annual Plan 1974–5*, p.8. To cite from the earlier *Fourth Five Year Plan 1970–5* (p.20): 'To increase the *per capita* consumption of foodgrains from 15.5 to 16.8 ounces per day; to ensure major increases in other items of essential consumption through a specific consumption plan: for instance, an increase in *per capita* consumption of 24 per cent in cotton textiles, 23 per cent in sugar and 20 per cent in edible oils.' (True, these are averages in terms of the entire population.)

14 Government of Malaysia (1971) *Second Malaysia Plan 1971-5*, Kuala Lumpur, p.42.
15 Government of the People's Republic of Bangladesh (1973) *The First Five Year Plan 1973-8*, Dacca, pp.9-10.
16 Government of Afghanistan (1967) *The Third Five Year Economic and Social Plan of Afghanistan 1967-71*, Kabul, p.27.
17 The Hashemite Kingdom of Jordan (1973) *Three Year Development Plan 1973-7*, Amman, p.15.
18 The United Republic of Tanzania (1969) *Second Five-Year Plan for Economic and Social Development 1 July 1969, 30 June 1974, vol. I: General Analysis*, Dar es Salaam, p.1.
19 Federal Republic of Nigeria (1975) *Third National Development Plan 1975-80*, vol. I, Lagos, p.29.
20 ibid., pp.30-1.
21 Republic of Ghana (1977) *Five Year Development Plan 1975/6-1979/80*, part I, Accra, p.27.
22 ibid., p.28.
23 The Republic of Uganda *Uganda's Third Five Year Development Plan 1971/2-1975/6*, Kampala, pp.5, 23, and 25.
24 Sierra Leone Government (1974) *National Development Plan 1974/5-1978/9*, Freetown, p.31.
25 ibid., p.39.
26 Somalia, Ministry of Information and National Guidance (1974) *Somalia's Five Year Plan 1974-8 — An Outline of the Economic Programme*, Mogadishu, p.3.
27 Ecuador (1972) *Plan Integral de Tranformacion y Desorrollo 1973-7*, Quito, p.4.
28 Discussing the 'link between employment and redistribution', Amartya Sen presents reasons 'why employment should be regarded as a vehicle of income distribution and why income cannot be redistributed more directly through taxation and fiscal policy'. ((1972) *Guidelines for Project Evaluation*, New York: United Nations, ch. 8)
29 For example, in Guatemala the target was to increase, during the 1975-9 Plan period 'the average family income in the lowest quartile of the population in real terms at an average annual rate of almost 5.5 per cent, as against the target of 4.5 per cent annual increase in the *per capita* income of the country as a whole'.

'In Panama the goal is to increase the share of total national income going to the poorest 20 per cent of the population from 1.6 per cent in 1970 to 4 per cent in 1981'.

Argentina, Costa Rica, and Venezuela have 'specified targets for increasing wages and salaries faster than total output or income'; 'wage policies' and related measures 'are expected to be effective in changing the distribution of income'.

An example may be cited from outside Latin America. In Algeria, the Plan foresees 'an annual increase of 9.5 per cent in the *per capita* consumption of representative rural families, as against the corresponding figure of 5.5 per cent for representative urban families';

Public Enterprise and Income Distribution

and 'an annual increase of 15.2 per cent in the *per capita* consumption of the poorest 10 per cent of the population, compared to the target of 7.6 per cent in the *per capita* consumption of the country as a whole'. ((1977) *Journal of Development Planning* no. 11: p.23).
30 The United Republic of Tanzania (1969) *Presidential Circular* no. 2.
31 Republic of Zambia (1971) *Second National Development Plan January 1972–December 1976*, Lusaka, p.194.
32 The Republic of Uganda *Uganda's Third Five Year Development Plan 1971/2–1975/6*, Kampala, p.25.
33 (1973) *Mid-Term Review of the Second Malaysia Plan 1971–5*, Kuala Lumpur, p.81. 'Foreign interests accounted for as much as 61 per cent of the total share capital invested in the corporate sector and . . . Chinese ownership accounted for about 22 per cent or just under 60 per cent of the total Malaysian share . . . . In industries in which foreign interests are not dominant, Chinese ownership of share capital is the highest, about 40 to 50 per cent. The ownership of share capital by Malays and Malay interests, on the other hand, is a mere 2 per cent of the overall total. A more balanced pattern in the ownership of assets in all sectors of the economy is necessary. The target of the Government is that within a period of 20 years, Malays and other indigenous people will own and manage at least 30 per cent of the total commercial and industrial activities of the economy in all categories and scales of operation'.
The Third Malaysia Plan (1976–80) reiterated as an objective the raising of 'the share of the Malays and other indigenous people in the ownership of productive wealth including land, fixed assets, and equity capital. The target is that by 1990, they will own at least 30 per cent of equity capital with 40 per cent being owned by other Malaysians'. ((1976) *Third Malaysia Plan 1976–80*, Kuala Lumpur, p. 49)
34 Bureau of Public Enterprises (1987) *Public Enterprises Survey, 1985–6*, New Delhi, p.2.
35 *The Gini coefficient* is a ratio of (a) the area on a graph that lies between the Lorenz curve and the egalitarian line (or line of perfect equality, which forms a 45 degree angle with both the x and y axes) to (b) the area of the entire triangle formed by the egalitarian line and the x and y axes. As a measure of income concentration, the Gini coefficient ranges from 0 to 1 — the larger the coefficient, the greater the inequality'. (The World Bank, Shail Jain (1975) *Size Distribution of Income — A Compilation of Data*, Washington, DC, p.xiv).

2. Employee incomes

1 A term frequently found in the public enterprise literature in developing countries.
2 'The Unions do not put the needs of the customer first despite their public statements of customer care . . . . The high wage settlements in 1980 showed that to be the case'. (Barlow, Sir William (1981) *The*

Notes

   Problems of Managing Nationalized Industries, London, p.10)
 3 For example, the level of benefits under the pension scheme of British Airways was considered 'unduly high', as compared with that in private sector companies. Hence it created a new scheme for fresh entrants, on privatization. (See Hyman, Howard (1988) 'Preparing for privatization: the financial aspects', in V.V. Ramanadham (ed.) *Privatization in the UK*, London)
 4 The data are drawn from the forthcoming book by Sauliniers, Alfred H. (1988) *Public Enterprises in Peru: The Military Years 1968–80*.
 5 National Board for Prices and Incomes (1969) *Top Salaries in the Private Sector and Nationalized Industries*, Report no. 107 (cmnd. 3970), London, p.32.
 6 ibid., p. 6.
 7 ibid., p.5.
 8 *Financial Times*, 17 August 1987, London.
 9 For instance, the emoluments of the Chairman of British Telecom rose to £172,000 by 1986 from the figure of £84,000 in its last year as a public enterprise. In 1981 the Chairman of Cable and Wireless received £11,291. It was privatized in that year. By 1986 his earnings rose to £238,843. (*Financial Times*, 19 July 1986 London)
10 Administrative Reforms Commission (1967) *Report on Public Sector Undertakings*, ch. VIII, New Delhi.
11 Forty-ninth Report on (1982) *Public Undertakings — Management and Control Systems*, New Delhi, pp.46–7. The Committee also quoted a witness stating that 'there are some concerns in which a Director gets Rs2,500 to Rs3,000 but a clerk will get Rs3,400 . . . . This is an inverted kind of discrimination which is coming in, that is, the more you rise to the top the less you get'.
12 *Report of the Working Party on Statutory Corporations and State-owned Companies*, parts I and II, Lagos, pp. 34–6.
13 ibid., pp. 35, 48.
14 For related comments, see Administrative Reforms Commission (of India), (1967) *Report on Public Sector Undertakings*, New Delhi, p. 77.
15 Reflections on Public Enterprises in Nigeria (1970) *The Report of the Conference on Public Enterprises in Nigeria*, Ahmadu Bello University, Zaria, p.45.
16 Federation of Nigeria (1960) *Report of Elias Commission of Inquiry into the Administration, Economics and Industrial Relations of the Nigerian Railway Corporation*, Lagos, p.41.
17 Government of Trinidad and Tobago (1969) *Third Five Year Plan 1969–73*, Port of Spain, p.44.
18 Naylor, G.W. (1966) *Report of Reconnaissance Mission to Ceylon in connection with State Industrial Corporations*, Colombo, p.23.
19 India, Committee on Public Undertakings (1967) (Third Lok Sabha) (Thirty Sixth Report) *Indian Oil Corporation Ltd*, New Delhi, p. 20.
20 ibid., pp.67–9.

21 India, Committee on Public Undertakings (1967) (Third Lok Sabha) (Thirty Seventh Report) *Hindustan Shipyard Ltd*, New Delhi, pp. 52–3.
22 India, Committee on Public Undertakings (1965) (Third Lok Sabha) (Eleventh Report) *Rourkela Steel Plant of Hindustan Steel Ltd*, New Delhi, pp. 31–2.
23 India, Committee on Public Undertakings (1973) (Fifth Lok Sabha) (Sixty Second Report) *Rural Electrification Corporation Limited*, New Delhi, p. 89.
24 India, Committee on Public Undertakings (1975) (Fifth Lok Sabha) (Sixty Third Report) *National Textile Corporation Limited*, New Delhi, p. 103.
25 Central Government (1970) *Audit Report (Commercial) 1970*, part IX, New Delhi, p.46.
26 *Report of the Comptroller and Auditor General of India* (1974) Union Government (Commercial), part III, *Hindustan Zinc Ltd*, New Delhi, p. 99.
27 *Report of the Comptroller and Auditor General of India* (1976) Union Government (Commercial), part III, (1976) *Neyveli Lignite Corporation Ltd*, New Delhi, pp. 161–3.
28 *British Steel* (Autumn 1975) London.
29 *British Steel Corporation: Ten Year Development Strategy* (1973) (cmnd. 5226), London: HMSO p. 12.
30 British Steel Corporation *Annual Report and Accounts 1973–4*, p. 20.
31 *First Report from the Select Committee on Nationalized Industries* (1973) Session 1972–7 *British Steel Corporation*, London: HMSO p. 14.
32 ibid., p. XXIV.
33 *First Report from the Select Committee on Nationalized Industries* (1977) Session 1976–7 *The Role of British Rail in Public Transport*, vol. II, London, pp. 54–5.
34 British Railways Board *Corporate Plan 1983–8*.
35 British Railways Board *Annual Report and Accounts 1986–7*, London, p. 32.
36 *The Economist*, 22 September 1979.
37 British Airways *Report and Accounts 1983–4*, London, p. 37.
38 Organization for Economic Co-operation and Development (1985/6) *Economic Surveys: Spain*, p. 35; (1985/6) *Portugal*, p. 26.
39 Das, P.K. (1965) in V.V. Ramanadham (ed.) *The Working of the Public Sector*, New Delhi, p. 235.
40 ibid., p. 237.
41 ibid., p. 231.
42 Trinidad and Tobago (1973) *Budget Speech 1973* by Hon. G.M. Chambers, Minister of Finance and Minister of Planning and Development, Port of Spain, p. 25.
43 Bureau of Public Enterprises (1976) *Annual Report on the Working of Industrial and Commercial Undertakings of the Central Government 1974–5*, vol. I, New Delhi.
44 Bureau of Public Enterprises (1983) *Public Enterprises Survey 1981–2*, vol. 1, New Delhi, p. 291.

45 Typical evidence comes from India. Defining the poverty line in terms of calories and cost of living, the *Sixth Five Year Plan 1980–5* (p. 51) observes that 'nearly 50 per cent of our population has been living below the poverty line continuously over a long period . . . . The majority of the poor live in the rural areas and belong to the categories of landless labourers, small and marginal farmers, rural artisans including fishermen, and backward classes and backward tribes'.
46 (1987) *Economic Survey 1986–7*, Islamabad, pp. 3–4.
47 An illustration of this situation comes from India. The Third Central Pay Commission highlighted that public enterprises were raising employee emoluments considerably despite the losses suffered by them.
48 For instance, referring to recent increases in coal prices in India, the Bureau of Public Enterprises, Ministry of Finance, referred to the 'revision of wages in the coal industry with effect from 1 January 1979' as a reason. ((1981) *Public Enterprises Survey 1979–80*, vol. 1, New Delhi, p. 207.)
49 (1975) *BSC (Industry) Ltd*.
50 For instance, the A.P. State Road Transport Corporation in India buys stores and batteries from small units, often under a scheme of price preference. Their poor quality not only raises the unit cost under these heads of expenditure, but also makes it necessary for the Corporation to buy a large volume in view of their short life.
51 (1984) *Economic Survey*, p. 52.
52 (1983) *Statistical Abstract*, pp. 229–33.
53 On the basis of data compiled from (1983) *Statistical Abstract*, pp.13, 239, and 250.
54 ibid.
55 ibid., p. 260.
56 (1984) *Economic Survey*, p. 77.
57 For instance, an Assistant Minister in the Office of the President was reported to have observed that cattle bought at 200 shillings or less fetched more than five times as much at the Kenya Meat Commission, and that the Commission would set up livestock-buying centres in remote areas of the district of Kitui. (*The Standard*, 1 June 1984, Nairobi), p. 8.

3. Pricing

1 For instance, the Rural Electrification Corporation in India has been advocating 'the most untenable proposition' that the State Electricity Boards should extend electricity supply to rural electric co-operatives 'at ridiculously low rates which would not even meet the incidence on account of wages, leave alone the actual cost of power on account of input'. (*Indian Express*, 3 January 1988, Hyderabad).
2 Fourth Report from the Select Committee on Nationalized Industries, op. cit., London, pp. xli–xlii.
3 This is a common legal provision. For instance, under the Laws of Barbados 'no public utility shall supply or furnish to any person any

service at rates which are unduly preferential or discriminatory'. (Ch. 282, part III, section 18).

4 For instance, in 1987 the Water and Power Development Authority of Pakistan charged a price of 39 pies per kWh up to 50 kWh of residential consumption, 46 pies for 51–150 kWh, 49 pies for 151–300 kWh and 64 pies for 301–600 kWh, and 89 pies above 600 kWh. Nepal Electricity Corporation have price differentials ranging from 44 to 90 paisa on domestic consumptions classified into ranges of 0–25, 25–100, 101–300, and above 300 kWh. A.P. State Electricity Board in India simply distinguishes between the first 100 kWh and beyond and charges, respectively, 45 paise and 50 paise. (The data are collected from the 1983 tariff schedules of these enterprises.)

5 See Vickrey, William S. (1980) 'Actual and potential pricing practices under public and private operation', in William J. Baumol (ed.) *Public and Private Enterprise in a Mixed Economy*, New York, p. 291.

6 Fourth Report from the Select Committee on Nationalized Industries, London, op. cit., pp.xli–xlii.

7 Department of Energy, United Kingdom (1976) *Energy Tariffs and the Poor*, London, pp. 4, 7, and 9.

8 Beesley, Michael and Littlechild, Stephen (1983) 'Privatization: principles, problems, and priorities', *Lloyds Bank Review*, London, July, p. 8.

9 *Further considerations relating to the British Telecommunications network and proposals to permit competition*, p. 6.

10 A usual case of such discriminations occurs on railways. For example 'concessions to certain groups may also be made for purely commercial reasons, reflecting their greater sensitivity to price and/or tendency to travel at times when demand is low, *helping to utilize otherwise empty capacity*. The half-fares for students and pensioners offered by British Rail fall into this category'. (First Report from the Select Committee on Nationalized Industries, session 1976–7 (1977) *The Role of British Rail in Public Transport*, vol. I, to lxxxiv)

11 The earlier cited *Energy Tariffs and the Poor* of the British Department of Energy referred, in the context of 'tariff changes proposed with a view to overcharging some consumers in order to benefit others', to 'the adverse implications for the industrial strategy and, as extra costs for industry would be passed on in higher prices for its products, for the counter-inflation policy and the international competitiveness of industry'. (paragraph 39, p. 14).

12 *Energy Tariffs and the Poor*, paragraphs 8 and 39, referring to the consumers' and consultative councils for electricity and gas.

13 *Energy Tariffs and the Poor*, op. cit., pp. 10 and 17.

14 First Report from the Select Committee on Nationalized Industries, Session 1976–7 (1977) *The Role of British Rail in Public Transport*, vol. I, London, p.lxxxii.

15 op. cit., p. lxxxiv.

16 (1984) *Buses*, (cmnd. 9300), London: HMSO, pp. 7, 8, and 35.

17 Planning Commission, Bangladesh (1979) *The First Five Year Plan 1973-8*, Dacca, p. 262.
18 For instance, the customer composition of 133 central government enterprises in India in 1982 reflected the predominance of sales to government departments, and to public enterprises — about 54 per cent of the total sales revenue. Exports accounted for about 7 per cent; and 'sales to others' for 39 per cent only. (*Report of the Comptroller and Auditor General of India* (1982) Union Government (Commercial), part I Introduction, New Delhi, p.xiii).
19 The Committee on Public Undertakings (1982-3) regretted that its recommendation of 1976 (in its 80th Report) that 'the public sector should have appropriate blend of bulk and formulations so as not to make losses but generate adequate margins on capital invested' did not receive prompt attention. The Ministry representative said: 'This imbalance is being corrected. But you cannot enter the market overnight. More and more formulations are being introduced. But it is very difficult to enter a well entrenched market because of severe competition'. The Committee also regretted that Hindustan Antibiotics Ltd 'does not have a fully organized Marketing Division'. ((1983) *Sixty-seventh Report on Hindustan Antibiotics Ltd*, New Delhi, pp. 31 and 45).
20 Glade, William P. (1979) *Entrepreneurship in the State sector: CONASUPO of Mexico*, no. 203, offprint series, Austin, TX: Institute of Latin American Studies.
21 Economic and Social Commission for Asia and the Pacific (1974) *Economic and Social Survey of Asia and the Pacific 1974*, Bangkok, p. 43.
22 First Report from the Select Committee on Nationalized Industries, Session 1976-7 (1977) *The Role of British Rail in Public Transport*, vol. II, minutes of evidence, London, p. 55-6.
23 ibid., pp. 65-6.
24 Vol. I, p. 59.
25 op. cit., vol. I, pp. lxxxvii-xc.
26 *The Economic Times*, 3 January 1988, Bombay.
27 Mittelholzer, C.I.V. (1970) *A talk on the operations of the Guyana Marketing Corporation*.
28 (1974) *National Development Plan 1974/5-1978/9*, Freetown, p. 39.
29 (1981) *Public Enterprises Survey 1979-80*, vol. 1, New Delhi, pp. 271 and 58.
30 (1983) *Government Sponsored Corporations 1981-2*, Islamabad, p. 195.
31 The Malays being relatively poor, the Government has devised a whole network of means for redressal. (65 per cent of Malay households are in poverty, as against 26 per cent of Chinese and 39 per cent of Indian householders.) Several public enterprises adopt policies that offer benefits of low prices on their outputs to the chosen ethnic group, the Malays: for example 'provision of advisory services at subsidized rates' by Majlis Amanah Rakyat (MARA), 'priority in the granting of credit facilities' by Bank Negara Malaysia, and 'reservation, at preferential rates (by 2 to 10 per cent) of government contracts to Malay

contractors'. ((1976) *Third Malaysia Plan*, Kuala Lumpur, pp. 5, 31, and 194).
32 *Sixth Five Year Plan 1980-5*, New Delhi, p. 81.
33 (1983) *Development Plan 1984-8* Nairobi, p. 59.
34 *Sixth Five Year Plan 1980-5*, New Delhi, p. 34.
35 Experts Advisory Cell, Ministry of Production, Pakistan (1984) *Annual Report 1982-3*, vol. I, Islamabad.
36 ibid., p. 250.
37 (1983) *Government Sponsored Corporations 1981-2*, Islamabad, p. 55.
38 Andhra Pradesh State Electricity Board, *Administration Report 1981-2*, pp. 74-83, Hyderabad.
39 For example, 45 paise per kWh of domestic consumption up to the first 100 units and 50 paise per kWh beyond; Rs50 per annum per HP of contracted or connected load, whichever is higher, in the case of agricultural low-tension consumption. (*The A.P. Gazetter Part II — Extraordinary*, 14 December 1983, Hyderabad).
40 To illustrate the basic point reference may be made to a recent study, by D.J. Storey, of the new firms established in the Cleveland area in the UK. He observed that 'the group, as a whole, purchased an average of 50 per cent of its inputs, by value, from local suppliers both at the date of establishment and in 1979'. ((1982) *Entrepreneurship and the New Firm*, London, p. 179).
41 Reference may be made to the study by Alejandro Rofman (1981) *Role of Public Enterprises in Regional Development in Latin America*, ICPE, pp. 29-30. 'Profits from the exploitation of natural resources are sent out of the region either in the form of material goods or as suppliers'. The two public enterprises in Patagonic region (Sierra Granda and Hidronor) 'increased the drain of basic resources towards more developed areas'.
42 Weiss, John (1980) *Practical Appraisal of Industrial Projects* (Application of Cost-Benefit Analysis in Pakistan), New York: United Nations, ch. 18.
43 For instance, John Weiss observes that an 'income weight of approximately 1.6 is required to justify the project' in Baluchistan, referred to in the text. That is, 'the Government would have to value income in the hands of residents of Baluchistan 60 per cent more highly than income going to either the Government itself or residents of other more developed regions'. (ibid., p. 111).

4. Deficits and Surpluses

1 The point may be illustrated by the Indian Government's decision to convert into an interest-free loan, in 1979, outstanding loans totalling Rs320 crores and non-plan loans of Rs75 crores for meeting the arrears of increased wages, repayment of loans and interest, and ways and means requirement up to the middle of July 1979. Further, the excise duty of Rs5 per tonne on non-coking coal and Rs7 per tonne on coking coal was discontinued from 18 July 1979. (Bureau of Public Enterprises

Notes

(1981) *Public Enterprises Survey 1979–80*, vol. 1, New Delhi, p. 20). The conversion of loans into equity is another common device in several countries. This may be illustrated from the Pakistan public enterprise sector, with reference to Pakistan Television Corporation Ltd, Utility Stores Corporation of Pakistan Ltd, and Mechanized Construction of Pakistan.

2 For a discussion on the point that the real costs of public enterprise operations are generally higher than are shown by their accounts, see Ramanadham, V.V. (1984) *The Nature of Public Enterprise*, London, ch. 12.
3 (1983) *Development Plan 1984–8*, Nairobi, p. 57.
4 *Sixth Five Year Plan 1980–5*, New Delhi, p. 51.
5 For example, the Food Corporation of India in respect of foodgrains, the State Trading Corporation of India Ltd in respect of edible oils, and the National Textile Corporation Ltd and the National Consumers Co-operative Federation in respect of 'controlled cloth'.
6 For example, State Civil Services Essential Commodities Corporations, in India, which will bear the burden of going to 'inaccessible areas, especially areas inhabited by the tribals and weaker sections of the community'. The Plan visualizes 'some subsidies . . . to retail outlets in such areas'. (*Sixth Five Year Plan 1980–5*, New Delhi, p. 83)
7 For a discussion of this issue, see Ramanadham, V.V. (1984) *The Nature of Public Enterprise*, London, part I 'The concept of public enterprise'.

5. The Aggregate Effects

1 The objectives included the following: to discourage concentration of wealth in the hands of a few; and to safeguard the interests of the small investor. 'Breaking the power of 22 (or so) industrial and commercial families was among the 'motivations which led to the tremendous and all-round growth of the public sector after 1972'. (Siddiqui, Anwar H. (ed.) (1979) *Management of Public Enterprises in Pakistan*, Lahore, pp. 5–6).
2 Short, R.P. (1983) *The Role of Public Enterprises: An International Statistical Comparison*, Washington, DC: IMF.
3 Trebat, Thomas J. (1980) *An Evaluation of the Economic Performance of Large Public Enterprises in Brazil, 1965–75*, Technical Papers Series no. 24, Austin, TX: Institute of Latin American Studies, pp. 11–12.
4 Trebat, Thomas J. *Brazil's State-owned Enterprises: A Case Study of the State as Entrepreneur*, p. 199.
5 Illustrative data on occupational and income distribution in twelve developing countries are available in Lecaillon, Jacques *et al.* (1984) *Income Distribution and Economic Development: An Analytical Study*, Geneva: ILO, p.55. Appendix 5.1 contains a graph based on the data.
6 As cited in Commonwealth Secretariat (1978) *Performance Evaluation of Public Enterprises* (Report of Seminar), Gaborone, p. 79.
7 Botswana *National Development Plan 1976–81*, Gaborone, p. 19.
8 See note 5 above.

6. Privatization and income distribution

1. For a full discussion, see Ramanadham, V.V. 'The Concept and Rationale of Privatization', paper submitted to the Seminar on privatization, at Templeton College, Oxford, in September 1987.
2. Third Report from the Committee of Public Accounts, Session 1985-6, (1985) *Sale of Government Shareholding in British Telecommunications plc*, London: HMSO, 35, p. ix-x.
3. See also Tenth Report from the Committee of Public Accounts, Session 1981-2, Department of Industry (1982) *Sale of Shares in British Aerospace; Sales of Government Shareholdings in other Publicly-owned Companies and in British Petroleum Ltd; Postponement of Payments:* 'All five sales were oversubscribed', London: HMSO, 189, p. x.
4. ibid., p. viii.
5. Seventeenth Report from the Committee of Public Accounts, Session 1983-4, Department of Transport, Department of Energy, (1984) *Sale of Government Shareholding in Publicly-owned Companies*, London: HMSO, 443, p. vi.
6. ibid., note 2, p. xii.
7. ibid., note 5, p. viii.
8. ibid., note 5, p. 3, Memorandum by the Comptroller and Auditor General.
9. Comment by National Audit Office, as cited in *Financial Times Survey on Privatization*, 16 September 1987, London, p.V.
10. Second Report from the Committee of Public Accounts, Session 1985-6, Departments of Transport, Trade and Industry and Energy, (1985) *Sale of Subsidiary Companies and Other Assets*, London: HMSO, 34, p. xi.
11. ibid., note 5, p. vii.
12. ibid., note 2, p. xiv.
13. ibid., note 3, p. vi.
14. Trades Union Congress *Stripping Our Assets*, London, p. 7. See also Hamish McRae: 'Hundreds of millions of public money are being distributed in a quite random way to people who happen to fill out forms in the papers and take a bit of money out of their building society account . . . . Their previous shareholders — the taxpayers — are having their assets sold too cheaply'. (*The Times*, 21 May 1987, London).
15. 'These shares would be sold in a manner that ensures wide dispersal of share ownership . . . . The objective is not to enhance the wealth of a few rich families. The objective is to bring about a widespread participation by the general public in the ownership of nationally-owned industries'. (*Budget Speech*, 1985-6, Islamabad (Pakistan), p. 14).
16. ibid., note, p. vii. See also note 14, p. 10.
17. ibid., note 3, pp. xi-xii. Some other instances of reduced numbers in the share registers may be cited. The number of small shareholders fell from 2.3 million to 1.4 million by March 1987 in British Telecom; in British Gas, from 4.5 million to 2.8 million; and in British Airways,

from 1.2 million to 420,000 by May 1987, (*Financial Times Survey on Privatization*, 16 September 1987, London, p. III).
18 Let us take, for illustration, the data relating to British Aerospace plc, as cited in a Report of the Committee of Public Accounts (1982). Statistical calculations of the skewness are vitiated by the fact that the last class interval of the data available there is open-ended: '1 million plus', with thirteen such shareholders. Even if we exclude that class and the capital they held from the aggregation, it can be deduced that no less than 80 per cent of the capital covered by those data (exclusive of HMG's shareholding and the shareholding of individual employees under the Employee Share Ownership Scheme) was held by the persons holding more than 10,000 shares each. (ibid., note 3, p. 15).
19 Overseas Development Institute *Briefing Paper*, September 1986, London.
20 *Financial Times*, 28 February 1987, London.
21 A scheme was designed, implying the issue of thirty-three free shares per employee under certain conditions, and of 'one free share' for every investment share purchased' 'under matching arrangements'. ibid., note 3, p. 15.
22 The BAA flotation provides for a free offer of forty-one shares to each eligible employee and a 'Matching Offer' of two free shares for each share purchased at the fixed price. (*BAA Offer for Sale*, 1987, p. 84).
23 House of Commons Debate, 9 January 1985, C. 490W.
24 (1987) *OECD Economic Surveys 1986–7: France*, Paris, p. 35.
25 ibid, p. 35.
26 (1986) *Privatization of the Water Authorities in England and Wales*, (cmnd. 9734), London: HMSO, p. 20.
27 Example may be cited of a subsidy from the Government proposed in the case of the WSPL's environmental services. (ibid., p.20).

7. Conclusion

1 For instance, it was observed by John Moore in *Why Privatize?* (1 November 1983) that 'public sector trade unions have been extraordinarily successful in gaining advantages for themselves in the pay hierarchy by exploiting their monopoly collective bargaining position . . . . Although it cannot be justified by productivity, most of the large industries' employee costs per employee increased faster than the national average over the period 1970–1 to 1982–3 and in many cases much faster, without corresponding increases in productivity'.
2 The Lecaillon *et al.* study cited already (chapter 5, note 5) contains useful illustrative data. For example, interesting contrasts are decipherable as between India and Chile, in respect of public expenditures on agriculture. (pp. 132 and 167).
3 'The public expenditure on energy, mining, industry and transport, and communications (including the necessary public works) has no effect on the inequality of incomes'. (ibid., p. 168).
4 ibid., p.179. For instance, in India 'there is a divorce between the

intentions of the Central Government which are to finance numerous schemes solely or primarily in the interest of the poor families, and the results obtained, since the share of the poor in the resources appropriated for the various activities referred to above amounts to less than half'. (p.132) The inference is from A. Gupta's study (1975) *Incidence of Central Government Expenditures in India*.

5 Bureau of Public Enterprises (1981) *Public Enterprises Survey 1979-80*, vol. 1, New Delhi, p. 211.

6 The Working Party on Government Expenditures cited 'the purchasing of maize through buying centres by the National Cereals and Produce Board' as an example of parastatals being 'instruments of public policy'. ((1982) *Report and Recommendations of the Working Party*, Nairobi, p. 44).

7 Glade, William P. (1977) *US Economic Relations with Latin America*, a special publication of the Institute of Latin American Studies, Austin, TX, p. 20.

8 Botswana (1977) *National Development Plan 1976-81*, Gaborone, p. 229.

9 As suggested in Ramanadham, V.V. (1984) 'Public Enterprise and Evaluation' (Lal Bahadur Shastri Memorial Lecture) *Studies in Public Enterprise*, London.

10 For instance, the Monopolies and Mergers Commission in the UK, which comes nearest to the desirable kind of agency vis-à-vis public enterprise, already goes into various aspects of costs and prices in such depth as to facilitate, under proper terms of reference, the processing of material directed to distributional appraisals.

Index

Afghanistan, 4
agriculture,
   dualism, 93-4
   low wages, 27, 92
Algeria, 115-16
ancillary industries, 32-3, 46
Andhra Pradesh State, 64, 93
   Electricity Board, 64, 120
   Road Transport Corporation, 67-82, 119
Argentina, 115
Associated British Posts Holding PLC 96

Baluchistan, 66, 122
Bangladesh, 4, 10, 49, 55-6
Barbados, 119-20
basic needs approach, 88, 92
Bharat Heavy Electricals Ltd, 19
Botswana, 92, 110
Brazil, 63, 92
British Aerospace, 97, 99, 125
British Airports Authority (BAA), 99, 125
British Airways, 20-1, 97, 117, 124-5
British Gas, 96-7, 124
British Rail, 20, 59-60, 120
British Steel Corporation, 15, 20, 30
British Steel Corporation (Industry) Ltd, 30
British Telecom, 52, 96, 97, 117, 124
Britoil, 96
budget deficits, 86, 100 (*see also* public debt)

budget surplus, 86

Cable and Wireless, 117
capital expenditures, 102-3
Cheran Transport Corporation, 75-6
Chile, 98, 125
Cleveland, UK, 122
CONASUPO, 59, 110
consumers, 47-8
   identification of poor, 49-51
   (*see also* prices)
co-operative organization, 93
Costa Rica, 115
cross-subsidizations, 52-3, 67-82, 105
current expenditure, 100-1, 103

Damodar Valley Corporation, 63
Das, P.K., 22
deficit financing, 85
deficit understatement, 83
deficits, 83-9, 91
   effects, 84-6
   nature, 83-4
   (*see also* surpluses)
distribution, 2
   employee incomes and, 25-32, 115
   government: direct expenditure, 87-9; policies, 108-10
   objectives of, 3-7
   privatization and, 95, 96-106
   public enterprise and, 6-7, 107-8; institutional

Index

aspects, 110-13
Dodgson, J., 20, 59-60
dualism, 27, 93-4

Economic and Social
  Commission for Asia and the
  Pacific, 59
Ecuador, 5
Egypt, 113
employee incomes, 13-46
  ancillary industries, 32-3;
    India, 46
  dualism, 27, 93-4
  generous incentives, 21-2
  high wages, 13-17
  implications for distribution
    25-32; beneficiaries, 26-7;
    yielders, 28-30
  Kenyan public enterprises,
    33-44
  Peru, 45
  social expenditures, 22-5
  surplus labour, 17-21
  (*see also* wages)
employee shareholding, 99, 125
equity, loans into, 123
Ethiopia, 113
Europe, 113 (*see also* under
  individual countries)
exchequer, 100-4

Fiji, 114
foreign investors, 104
France, 95, 97, 101, 102

Ghana, 5, 6, 49
Ghee Corporation of Pakistan
  Ltd, 60
Gini coefficient, 10-12, 116
government,
  direct distribution, 87-9
  distributional policies, 108-10;
    and public enterprise,
    110-13
  subsidies, 53-6, 84-6, 105
growth, 91-2
Guatemala, 115
Guyana, 49
  Marketing Corporation, 60

Harnai Woollen Mills, 63
Hindustan Antibiotics Ltd, 58,
  121
Hindustan Shipyard Ltd, 19
Hindustan Steel Ltd, 19
Hindustan Zinc Ltd, 19
holding companies, 49

identification of poor consumers,
  49-51
incentives 21-2, 26
income (*see* employee income)
India,
  Administrative Reforms
    Commission, 16
  ancillary industries, 46
  basic needs, 88
  Boothalingam Committee, 16
  Bureau of Public Enterprises,
    22, 25, 46, 61
  Committee on Public
    Undertakings (CPU), 14, 16,
    19, 121
  cost understatement, 122
  cross-subsidizations, 67-82
  distributional objectives, 3
  Food Corporation of, 61, 110,
    123
  Housing and Urban Development
    Corporation, 62-3
  merit consumption, 52
  missed targets, 125-6
  National Consumers Cooperative
    Federation, 123
  National Textile Corporation
    Ltd, 123
  overtime payments, 22
  poverty line, 119
  pricing, 60, 61, 62-3, 119, 120,
    intermediate goods, 121
  public distribution system, 61
  public enterprise, 6, 7, 123
  regional development, 63, 64
  social expenditures, 23-5
  State Civil Services Essential
    Commodities Corporations,
    123
  State Electricity Boards, 52, 60, 64
  State Trading Corporation, 123

Index

surplus labour, 18-20
wages, 14, 16, 25, 117, 119;
  dualism, 27
  (*see also* Andhra Pradesh;
  Tamilnadu)
Indian Oil Corporation (IOC), 19
inflation, 85-6
input policies, 65, 112
Instituto Reconstruzione Industriale
  (IRI), 63
intermediate goods, 56-8
International Monetary Fund (IMF),
  91
investment in public enterprise, 7-12
Iran, 4
Italy, 63, 98

Jamaica, 95
Jordan, 4

Kenya,
  basic needs, 88
  Meat commission, 44, 119
  National Cereals and Produce
    Board, 44, 60, 110, 126
  National Irrigation Board, 44
  privatization, 95
  regional development, 63
  wages in public enterprise, 14,
    33-44
Kuwait, 4

labour, surplus, 17-21, 26, 30
Latin America, 10, 110, 115 (*see
  also* under individual countries)
leakages, 65-6, 87
Lecaillon, J., 93, 109, 125
loans, 122-3
low prices, 48-9, 62 (*see also*
  prices)

Madagascar, 113
Malaysia, 4, 6
  ownership of assets, 116
  sectoral pricing, 61, 121-2
managers,
  as distributional arbiters, 50-1,
    88-9, 108-9
  incentives, 22

salaries, 14, 15-17
McRae, H., 124
merit consumption, 51-2
Mexico, 59
monopolies, 13, 105-6
Monopolies Commission, 112
Moore, J., 125
Morocco, 114
multiplier effect, 65

Nepal Electricity Corporation, 120
Neyveli Lignite Corporation Ltd, 20
Nigeria,
  distributional objectives, 3, 4-5
  Elias Commission, 18
  surplus labour, 18
  Working Party on Statutory
    Corporations and State-owned
    Companies, 16-17

Organisation for Economic
  Co-operation and Development
  (OECD), 21
overtime, 22

Pakistan,
  distributional objectives, 3, 4,
    114
  Economic Reforms Order, 90
  Equity Participation Fund, 64
  Experts Advisory Cell, 63
  Industrial Development
    Corporation, 63
  loans into equity, 123
  pricing, 59, 60, 61, 120
  public enterprises, 123
  public investment and Gini
    coefficient, 10-12
  regional development, 63-4, 66
  shareholding, 98, 124
  Utility Stores Corporation, 61
  wages, 27
  Water and Power Development
    Authority, 64, 120 (*see also*
    Baluchistan)
Pallavan Transport Corporation, 75
Panama, 115
Peru, 14, 45, 95
Portugal, 21

129

Index

poverty, 27, 92-3, 119
price discriminations, 29, 119-20
   distributional, 48, 51-2, 53, 64
prices, 47-82, 107, 112
   distributional, 47-9
   dual, 61
   employee incomes policies, 28-30
   final consumers, 49-56; cross-subsidizations, 52-3, 67-82, 84; government subsidies, 53-6
   intermediate goods, 56-8
   low, 48-9, 62
   regional development, 63-7
   sectoral, 58-63
   uniform, 73, 74, 76
private enterprise,
   employee incomes, 15-16, 27
   pricing, 29-30
privatization, 95-106
   concept, 95-6
   exchequer implications, 100-4
   long-term implications, 104-6
   sale implications, 96-9
Pryke, R., 20, 59-60
public debt, 86 90-1, 101-2, 103
public enterprise,
   composition, 91-3
   distribution and, 107-8, 110; institutional aspects, 110-13
   investment in, 7-12
   levels, 2
   size, 90-1
Public Enterprise Commission, 112
public expenditures, 109, 125

regional development, 63-7
reserves, 84
Rofman, A., 122
Royal Nepal Airlines Corporation, 52
Rural Electrification Corporation, 19, 119

St Gobain, 97
Sealink, 97
secondary effects, 56-8, 65-6, 92, 122

selectivity, 109
Sen, A., 115
shareholding, 98-9, 104, 124-5
Sierra Leone, 5, 6, 60
   Marketing Board, 60
small shareholders, 98-9, 104, 124-5
social expenditures, 22-5, 26
Somalia, 5, 113
Spain, 21
Sri Lanka, 3, 18, 95
Storey, D.J., 122
sub-markets, 61-2
Sudan, 49, 113
surplus labour, 17-21, 26, 30
surplus overstatement, 83
surpluses, 29, 65, 83, 91 (*see also* deficits)
Syria, 113

Tamilnadu, 75-6
Tanzania, 4, 6, 49
taxes,
   deficits and, 29, 85, 86, 91
   privatization and, 100
textile mills, 'sick', 19
trade unions, 125
Trades Union Congress (TUC), 97
Trinidad and Tobago, 18, 22

Uganda, 5, 6, 49
uniform prices, 73, 74, 76
United Kingdom (UK),
   Department of Energy, 51, 120
   Department of Transport, 96
   Electricity Council, 50, 51
   Monopolies and Mergers Commission, 126
   National Board for Prices and Incomes, 15
   National Bus Company, 52
   price concessions, 50, 51, 54, 55, 59-60
   privatization, 95, 96-7, 98, 100, 105; employee shareholding, 99
   Public Service Obligation (PSO) payments, 54
   secondary effects, 122

Index

surplus labour, 20-1
wages, 15-16
Water Service Public Limited Companies (WSPL), 105, 125
United Nations, 114

Venezuela, 12, 63, 115

wages,
   distribution and, 65, 107, 112, 125
   high, 13-17, 26
   increases, 29, 30-1, 119

Kenyan public enterprise, 33-44
lowest, 27
Peru, 45
(*see also* employee incomes)
Weiss, J. 122
windfall gains, 98
workers, incentives and, 22
World Bank, 10

Yemen, 113

Zambia, 6